Rigged

MANCHESTER
1824

Manchester University Press

POLITICAL ETHNOGRAPHY

The Political Ethnography series is an outlet for ethnographic research into politics and administration and builds an interdisciplinary platform for a readership interested in qualitative research in this area. Such work cuts across traditional scholarly boundaries of political science, public administration, anthropology, social policy studies and development studies and facilitates a conversation across disciplines. It will provoke a re-thinking of how researchers can understand politics and administration.

Previously published titles

The absurdity of bureaucracy: How implementation works   Nina Holm Vohnsen

Politics of waiting: Workfare, post-Soviet austerity and the ethics of freedom
Liene Ozoliņa

Diplomacy and lobbying during Turkey's Europeanisation: The private life of politics
Bilge Firat

Dramas at Westminster: Select committees and the quest for accountability
Marc Geddes

Rigged

Understanding 'the economy'
in Brexit Britain

Anna Killick

Manchester University Press

Published by Manchester University Press
Altrincham Street, Manchester M1 7JA
www.manchesteruniversitypress.co.uk

British Library Cataloguing-in-Publication Data
A catalogue record for this book is available from the British Library

ISBN 978 1 5261 4516 1 hardback
ISBN 978 1 5261 5927 4 paperback

First published 2020

The publisher has no responsibility for the persistence or accuracy of URLs for any external or third-party internet websites referred to in this book, and does not guarantee that any content on such websites is, or will remain, accurate or appropriate.

Typeset by Newgen Publishing UK

Contents

Figures

Tables

Series editor's preface

Ethnography reaches the parts of politics that other methods cannot reach. It captures the lived experience of politics, the everyday life of political elites and street-level bureaucrats. It identifies what we fail to learn, and what we fail to understand, from other approaches. Specifically:

1 it is a source of data not available elsewhere
2 it is often the only way to identify key individuals and core processes
3 it identifies 'voices' all too often ignored
4 by disaggregating organisations, it leads to an understanding of 'the black box', or the internal processes of groups and organisations
5 it recovers the beliefs and practices of actors
6 it gets below and behind the surface of official accounts by providing texture, depth and nuance, so our stories have richness as well as context
7 it lets interviewees explain the meaning of their actions, providing an authenticity that can only come from the main characters involved in the story
8 it allows us to frame (and reframe, and reframe) research questions in a way that recognises that our understandings about how things work around here evolves during the fieldwork
9 it admits surprises – of moments of epiphany, serendipity and happenstance – that can open new research agendas
10 it helps us to see and analyse the symbolic, performative aspects of political action

Despite this distinct and distinctive contribution, ethnography's potential is rarely realised in political science and related disciplines. It is considered an endangered species or at best a minority sport. This series seeks to promote the use of ethnography in political science, public administration and public policy.

The series has two key aims.

1. To establish an outlet for ethnographic research into politics, public administration and public policy.

2. To build an interdisciplinary platform for a readership interested in qualitative research into politics and administration. We expect such work to cut across the traditional scholarly boundaries of political science, public administration, anthropology, organisation studies, social policy and development studies.

We negotiate our way through everyday life with many taken-for-granted assumptions about the worlds in which we live. Our language is littered with words we never unpack, such as class, gender and ethnicity. One such word is the 'economy'. What do we mean when we use the word? Do we refer to the abstract world of the economist with its notion of gross domestic product (GDP) and balance of payments? Or do we refer to the lived economy of work, unemployment and welfare benefits? Anna Killick's book asked people living in a city on the south coast of England 'how do you understand the term "the economy" when you hear politicians and media commentators talk about it?' She conducted her fieldwork between 2016 and 2018. She focused on two districts: the lower- income Hill district and the higher- income Church district, interviewing 60 people from diverse social and occupational backgrounds. She interviewed people aged 18 to 80, and equal numbers of men and women.

As with all the books in this series, I am impressed by the intrepid ethnographer. Anna Killick tramped the streets of the southern city. Come hail or storm, or more commonly rain, she knocked on the doors of total strangers with apprehension clutching at her stomach, wondering about her possible reception. Surfing waves of uncertainty is the fieldworker's lot and she successfully rode her personal Mavericks time after time. With consummate skill she gained the confidence of her interviewees, who talked freely and at length about the ups and downs of their working life. She demonstrates there can be no substitutes for 'being there' if we want to understand other people's lives.

The core argument of this book is that there is an 'official' version of the economy, but not everyone understands this version and some people resist it. Different groups of people understand the term differently. People saw the economy through the spectacles of their own experiences. Low-income participants saw the economy as an intense struggle and were bitter about how disproportionately austerity affected them. They did not believe George Osborne's claim that 'we're all in this together' because they experienced high levels of job insecurity and repeated cuts in welfare benefits. High-income participants were comfortable with the term, believing they benefited from 'our economy'; it was a positive force. Political beliefs, education, gender and age shape people's understandings of the economy, but personal economic experiences had the greatest influence.

Anna Killick's insightful book illustrates the long-standing merits of an ethnographic approach. She identifies 'voices' all too often ignored. She gets behind the surface of official understandings. She provides depth and nuance, so her stories have richness. She can do so because she lets interviewees explain the meaning of their actions. In short, she provides an authentic account. We believe in the bitterness of the main characters involved in the story. We are on their side about the rigged economy. Like all good ethnography, she opens the consciousness of one group to the lives of another. Such empathy is as important as it is rare when neighbour is pitted against neighbour in our troubled era.

Professor R. A. W. Rhodes
University of Southampton
Series editor

Preface

This book was born in history lessons in a Dorset comprehensive school. When teenagers are learning about why Britain invaded Egypt in 1882 or the Nazi Party came to power in Germany, they do not instinctively separate out the 'economic' reasons. But the exam boards require them to do that and, as their teacher, I found myself training them. I was often reduced to simplistic injunctions such as 'if it's to do with money, it's economic!' For many of the girls in particular, once grasped, 'the economy' seemed a technical phenomenon that felt alien to them. They would say they preferred social or political history. As the neoliberal decades progressed, when I was talking to students in politics lessons, I also noticed how readily they seemed to accept that the economy exerted a logic or force that no human could resist. So, when I decided to leave the classroom to conduct doctoral research, I started with the intention of researching into how young people understood the term 'the economy', specifically in political contexts, trying to decide whether or how to vote. But while I could immerse myself in the classics, reading Marx, Polanyi or Geertz or more recent anthropology and heterodox economics works, I could not find recent research by political scientists into how people understood the term – in Walter Lippmann's words, 'the pictures that went through their minds'. Katharine Cramer's study of why so many rural residents of Wisconsin vote for politicians who oppose spending programmes they will benefit from came closest, as she was trying to get to the bottom of what she called a 'politics of resentment', where the cultural and economic are entwined. But apart from the excellent work by Lisa Mckenzie on why some working-class people voted Leave, there was no British equivalent. So I decided to research all age groups, from 18 to 80, and to find people to interview from as broad a range of backgrounds as possible.

I had planned to research understanding of the economy before Leave won the June 2016 referendum. So my fieldwork, which began just after, took on a heightened degree of emotion as 'the economy' became perhaps more of a battle ground than it has ever been. I have called this book a study of understanding in Brexit Britain because the fieldwork was conducted between July 2016 and early

2018 and participants wanted to talk about Brexit a lot. But it did also surprise me how much anyone over thirty also talked so historically – about Thatcher's deindustrialisation or the 2008 crisis. I hope the book says something about how people's understanding of the economy may change, but be quite slow to do so.

I was lucky that so many people in my chosen city invited me in to their homes. Talking about 'the economy' does not come naturally to people. On the doorsteps some even said to me it would be worse than talking about politics. But they were generous enough to give me their time. And sometimes, at the end of them picking the economic bits out of their life stories, the housing and jobs, the shoes with paper in or bread for tea, the bailiffs or mortgage advisers, they would say how surprised they were to have enjoyed the experience and how interesting or important a subject this was.

To the reader, if you are mainly interested in the substantive message about what the participants think about the economy, you can skim Chapter 2 and the Appendix, which are mainly for those interested in interpretivist ethnographic methods. Some of the findings are subject-themed, such as on employment in Chapter 3, debt and austerity in Chapter 4 and 'Brexit' issues of trade and migration in Chapter 5. Chapter 6 explores understanding of 'the economy' as a whole. The final two chapters analyse and conclude. The concluding chapters may at times seem tentative. If they do, it is because I do not think we have done enough of this kind of talking to people; more of this kind of research needs to be done as a matter of urgency, lest we as political scientists start to become too distant from people at the same time as we pronounce upon their motives.

My first thanks are to the students I taught; if they listen, you teach your teachers more than you know. You have grown up in what many would describe as a neoliberal economy and it has culminated in recent years in the beast of Brexit that turns most things upside-down. You may fear whether you will get jobs, or, as concern for the environment increases, where the economy fits into that. My second thanks go to the participants in this book. I hope I have represented what you said accurately. Some of you said you wanted to send a message and I hope I have delivered it. I am very grateful for the support I had from Rod Rhodes, who also helped me turn this into a book; to Matthew Watson and Deborah Mabbett; to those in the economics literacy world I had contact with, like Ali Norrish; and to all the political economists and other political writers who have inspired this. Last, I thank my immediate and extended family, who do not seem to me to be that split on the subject of 'the economy', even though they are split in so many fascinating ways on the subject of Brexit.

What is 'the economy'?

In a city on the south coast of England one evening, just after the 2016 referendum on the European Union, Diane talks about the economy at the offices where she works as a cleaner. She is on the top floor in a corridor overlooking the housing estate where she grew up and where her mother still lives. She is in her early thirties, married with four children. She is composed and, at times, reticent. She describes how just before the 2008 financial crisis her husband was earning high wages as a painter and decorator so they decided to buy a house. A few months later the crash happened and his earnings dipped almost straight away. They 'struggled on' trying to make the payments but realised they would have to sell at a loss to avoid repossession. Nearly ten years later she is working two minimum-wage jobs, as cleaner and care home assistant, having to work 'vice versa' with her husband. 'Vice versa' means that because childcare is too expensive, when she is at work he looks after the children, and when she comes home he leaves for work. They are still thousands of pounds in debt, in a debt management plan, chipping away at it. She describes the debt as a 'black hole' and says they will never go back 'that way' to homeownership again.

Some weeks later, a few streets away from where Diane works, four women meet in one of their houses. They are close friends and two of them are mother and daughter. When they are talking about how people on low incomes or benefits like them manage, Linda explains that she knows people, alluding to her daughter Misha sitting opposite, who prioritise spending their last cash on hair extensions rather than food. Misha replies that when she asks her mother or brother to lend her £20 for hair extensions they say no, whereas if she gets the extensions done and then asks them to lend her money for her children's food, they say yes. She adds: 'That's the way I run my economy!' Misha later admits she does not think she will ever get out of debt or stop going further in.

In the autumn, in the same city a mile to the south, Rachel, sitting at her kitchen table, says her upbringing was frugal but secure. As a child she 'knew that there was money behind us, if that makes sense, it just wasn't an obvious thing'. She is still frugal and disapproves of debt, having no debts apart from her mortgage. However, she knows a lot about finances and has a small pot of savings she invests.

> I think I've reached a stage where I know what [money] I have. I know where it is... I do have a few little shares of my own that I kind of speculate a bit on. That's money that I know if I lose it, that's okay.

Rachel says she is interested in 'the economy' and 'follows' it. She follows interest rates, exchange rates and the fortunes of the private sector where her husband works.

There is a gulf between Diane and Misha's economic experiences on the one hand and Rachel's on the other. Diane and Misha were forced to move to the cheaper edge of the council house estate where they grew up, into the insecure private rented sector. By definition, waged work is minimum-waged work. They are both in debt. In contrast, Rachel is financially secure living in a house worth several times what she paid for it and drawing on pensions in early retirement. Diane and Misha experience 'the economy' tangentially but powerfully. It hit Diane directly in 2008 and it hits them both, in the shape of minimum-wage rates, in-work benefits and social services, on a day-to-day basis. In contrast, Rachel actively *follows* 'the economy', speculating on it.

In Brexit Britain, talk about 'the economy' dominates. From the 2016 referendum on membership of the European Union until the 2019 election, the main theme was how much 'no deal' or softer versions of Brexit would damage the economy (UK Government 2018). At the time of writing, these arguments about the economic effects of different future relationships with the European Union look like they will continue to run even after the decisive Conservative election victory of 2019.

What people believe about 'the economy' is therefore key to understanding politics. The orthodox view is that people believe 'the economy' is more important than any other issue in the sense that they vote for the policies that will make either their households or the country better off (Duch and Stevenson 2008; Lewis-Beck et al. 2012, 2013). Some political economists and political behaviour scholars believe that, broadly speaking, 'the economy' and economic issues are still the most important issues in politics. They argue that in the 2016 referendum, low-income Leave voters may not always have voted for what they believed would make them better off, but they were motivated by issues that could more broadly be considered economic: anger at the faltering recovery from the 2008 crisis, rising economic inequality and austerity, feeling shut out from the benefits of globalisation or, even more broadly, alienated by years of the needs of 'the economy' being presented as trumping everything else (Berry 2016; Colantone and Stanig 2016; Dorling 2016).

However, an increasingly dominant narrative is that those who believe 'the economy' is important support Remain but that 'cultural' goals drive some to support Leave even though it will cause 'economic self-harm' (Legrain n.d.; Owen and Walter 2017). This narrative stems in part from polling, such as that done in the weeks before the 2016 referendum by the British Election Study, asking people what 'the most important issue' was in helping them decide how to vote. Overwhelmingly, those intending to vote Leave came up with the word 'immigration', while those intending to vote Remain came up with the word 'economy' (Prosser et al. 2016). This division is echoed in the title of John Curtice's (2016) analysis of the referendum result and in many other publications and media commentary as 'two poles'. Since 2016, attaching importance to 'the economy' seems to have become a fault line or cleavage in its own right. In the 2019 general election, a greater proportion of working-class people voted Conservative than Labour (McDonnell and Curtis 2019), despite the fact that Labour claimed to offer more economic policies directed at them. Some argue that this is not a temporary phenomenon, that whatever components go to make up 'Brexit identities', they may be stronger than party political ones (Hobolt et al. 2018), reflecting a deep change in the nature of British politics.

But is it the case that Remain supporters, with disproportionately high incomes and having spent more years in education, care more about 'the economy' than Leave supporters? In this book I argue that we cannot answer questions about how important people believe 'the economy' is if we do not know what they understand by that term in the first place. What goes through people's minds when they hear politicians talk about 'the economy'? What goes through their minds when surveys ask them how much importance they attach to it? Do people as diverse as Rachel, Diane and Misha understand the term 'the economy' in the same way as each other or in the same way as the political scientists asking and interpreting survey questions understand it? Are understandings of this term changing? It may seem common sense that everyone understands 'the economy' is 'to do with money' just as society is 'to do with people'. But such definitions are too shorthand. In the words of one of the founders of public opinion studies, Walter Lippmann, we need to know what pictures go through people's minds when they hear terms and how the pictures vary (1922:18). In the case of the pictures that go through people's minds when they hear the term 'the economy', we know surprisingly little.

Conducting ethnographic fieldwork starting just after the 2016 referendum and continuing into 2018, I asked: how do you understand the term 'the economy' when you hear politicians and media commentators talk about it? The following chapters are about sixty people living in a city on the south coast of England and how they see 'the economy', how it links with their lives and what they understand about different aspects of it, such as trade or the economic effects of migration. The fieldwork was conducted in the two years following the 2016 referendum but reveals more of an underlying understanding of 'the economy'. It was conducted in one city but includes people from as many backgrounds as possible: the marginalised *and* the frequently heard, men and women, old and young. It was conducted with an open mind about what understandings might emerge and whether there would be patterns in understandings. It is part of a broader movement to engage in the messy and often inconclusive business of exploring meanings. It does not aim to provide direct answers to why people vote the way they do, but it does aim to enhance understanding of how they might be picturing 'the economy' as they do it and, in doing so, raises some questions about taking categories like 'the economy' and 'economic' for granted.

Understandings of 'the economy'

How do people understand what the term 'the economy' means? Tim Mitchell has said 'the economy' is a 'concept that seems to resist analysis' (1998:84). At the same time, it is a taken-for-granted concept with many assuming people instinctively understand it in the same way. If we take the case of mainstream politicians, who dominate the media presentation of 'the economy' and frame what people like Rachel, Diane and Misha will hear if they come across that media commentary, this sense that everyone out there understands what they mean by the term 'the economy' comes across in a powerful way.

The official version: taking 'the economy' for granted

Over the period when the fieldwork for the book was conducted, from the 2016 EU referendum through a general election and the Brexit negotiations into 2018, politicians from all parties were constantly talking about 'the economy' and urging people to vote for the sake of it. Moore and Ramsay's analysis of media coverage during the referendum campaign shows 'the economy' was 'the most referenced political issue' (2017:40). There are some differences in how leading Leave politicians, including Nigel Farage, approached it. He tended not to raise 'the economy' proactively but concentrated on criticising economic experts and 'Project Fear' or linking any concerns about 'the economy' to the problem of immigration.[1] But analysis of public announcements by politicians from the Labour and Conservative Parties[2] indicates they raise 'the economy'

[1] From a Nexis search conducted on 26 January 2018 of all UK newspapers in the period 1 April–23 June 2016 for references to 'Farage' and 'the economy'. See also Moore and Ramsay (2017).
[2] Extracts selected from the top 20 results in two separate Nexis searches, conducted on 27 September 2018, searching for UK national newspaper references for 'Cameron' OR 'Osborne' OR 'Hammond' OR 'Corbyn' OR 'McDonnell' AND 'the economy' from 1 April 2016 until 27 September 2018 and again on 1 April 2019 for the preceding six months, substituting 'May' for 'Osborne'.

more proactively, and that in some respects they talk about it in the same way, not just in the 2016 campaign but also in the years since, including in talk about 'the economy' not related to Brexit.

The two key elements in the understanding of Labour and Conservative politicians are that 'the economy' is a term that everyone understands – a neutral phenomenon – and that it is distinct from the rest of human life.

First, despite advocating different economic policies, Conservative and Labour politicians use 'the economy' as an *umbrella term* and often do not feel the need to define it further. In April 2016, according to Conservative Chancellor George Osborne spearheading the Remain campaign, 'the economy' is something that can 'grow' and contract. He says 'it's good news that Britain continues to grow, but there are warnings today that the threat of leaving the EU is weighing on our economy'. He describes 'the economy' as 'strong' in the speech, pleading 'let's not put the strong economy we're building at risk, and vote to Remain on June 23' (Dathan 2016). In some speeches Osborne spells out what 'the economy' encompasses – 'people's income and jobs' (Settle 2016) – but politicians often dispense with such detail and Prime Minister David Cameron backs Osborne on the same day by saying simply 'it is right; leaving the EU would pose major risks for the UK economy' (Settle 2016).

In his speech to the Conservative Party conference in October 2016 the subsequent Conservative Chancellor Philip Hammond warns of a 'roller-coaster' ride for Britain's economy and promises to 'grow the economy', contrasting it now with its state in 2010 at the end of the Labour period in government when it 'looked out for the count' (Hammond 2016). But despite contesting claims about the effects of Conservative economic policies, Labour politicians adopt the same approach of using 'the economy' as an umbrella term that does not require defining. In June 2016 Labour leader Jeremy Corbyn warns, 'it's not good for our communities or your families if we are running a weak economy' (Swinford 2016) and, just before the 2017 general election, Labour Shadow Chancellor John McDonnell spells out his vision for 'a big deal to upgrade the economy' (Bartlett 2017).

Second, politicians' talk about '*the* economy' uses the definite article combined with images of growth or contraction and gives the impression of something that is a phenomenon of itself and separate from the rest of human activity. This links with the idea that 'the economy' is about impersonal forces, the demand and supply of goods and money. As Hammond argues, in October 2016, it is 'post-Brexit Britain's economy' that faces a 'daunting challenge' (Wilkinson 2016), as if it is not us that do.

This approach to the use of the term 'the economy' has not changed since the referendum. For instance, in February 2019 Labour economic spokesperson John McDonnell says his party's support for any Brexit deal will be contingent on it protecting 'jobs and the economy' (ITV 2019) while supporters of Prime Minister May's deal say it will do just that (Thomson and Sylvester 2019).

The core argument of this book is that there is an 'official' version, but not everyone understands the term 'the economy' as presented in that version, that some people resist it and that different groups of people seem to understand the term in different ways. At least two broad understandings emerge from the field-work, and they dominate the rest of this book, but, before setting out what they are, I want to trace back to the roots of the official version and alternatives to it, because doing so helps to contextualise what emerged from the fieldwork.

I argue that the official version presented by mainstream politicians is echoed by the media and economists and also many political scientists, those interpreting how important 'the economy' is to people when they act politically. In essence, even though Labour politicians like John McDonnell advocate socialist economic policies and draw on heterodox and neo-Marxist economics (2017), they frame 'the economy' in a way that is similar to their Conservative counterparts and based in the sense of 'the economy' as an umbrella term for a universally understood phenomenon that is distinct from the human sphere.

The formal economy

Before the late nineteenth century, economists might have spoken, as Adam Smith did, about an invisible hand of the market, but they saw the economic sphere, where people trucked and bartered, as linked with other human spheres like politics and society (Smith 1999, 2000). However, late nineteenth-century 'marginalist' economists like William Jevons and Carl Menger put the discipline of economics on a more formal footing. They developed 'scientific' laws that they argued governed the operation of economies, such as the iron law of wages and the theory of comparative advantage (originally proposed by David Ricardo [1817] 1996; see also Watson 2005, 2012). Loren Lomasky describes these laws as 'below surface'; they cannot be observed or understood by an untrained eye (2008:471). Abstractions and models are necessary to learn how they might apply to real-world conditions. Only trained economists, drilled in the laws until they lose their more 'common sense' thinking, can fully understand how 'the economy' works. These economists' 'economy' consisted of impersonal forces, distinct from the human. They were the first to use the definite article that is now so instinctive for politicians, talking about 'the economy'.

In the twentieth century the marginalist economists became dominant to the extent that to this day the majority of economists describe themselves as neoclassical and accept the fundamentals such as the laws, even if they some-times disagree on other aspects such as whether to adopt Keynesian or monet-arist approaches (for a critique see Earle et al. 2017). They became influential within the civil service and government. It also suited politicians to talk about 'the economy', in the twentieth century increasingly synonymous with 'the national economy' (Tooze 1998), as two world wars and technological and industrial advances increased their ambition to control more aspects of people's lives (Mitchell 2008a; Tomlinson 2017).

The formal or neoclassical approach of treating 'the economy' as a universally understood term for impersonal forces also permeates some fields in political science. Like mainstream politicians, many political scientists seem to assume people understand what 'the economy' means, treating it as a given. For instance, political scientists routinely phrase survey questions with the term 'the economy' in them as if it is just an umbrella term that does not need to be defined further. The British Election Study (2017) asks simply:

How well do you think the present government has handled the economy?
Do you think immigration is good or bad for Britain's economy?

Some political scientists even argue most people also have the same goals for 'the economy'. They want it to be 'healthy' or 'growing' and will vote for the political party that has the best reputation for 'managing' it without necessarily applying the same partisan scrutiny to their economic policies as to their other polices (Stokes 1992:143). However, I argue that the participants in the fieldwork for this book suggest that people do not share such a common sense of what 'the economy' is or should be and that any common understanding that did exist may have declined in recent years, leading to people approaching political scientists' questions about 'the economy' with a growing dissonance.

Some economists and political scientists do research aspects of people's understanding of 'the economy', such as what 'healthy' or 'growing' mean (Stiglitz et al. 2010), or whether rising economic inequality and problems related to the 2008 crash have modified how much of a 'valence' issue 'the economy' is (Borges et al. 2013). However, generally, political scientists have not done as much empirical research into the pictures that go through people's minds when they hear the term 'the economy' or answer political scientists' survey questions about it as they have some other concepts, such as immigration (Wong 2007; Ford 2011; Skey 2011; Blinder 2015; Tonkiss 2016; Pilkington 2016). Political scientists have tended to leave open study of what 'the economy' means to anthropologists and economic sociologists and psychologists (Moscovici 1988; Roland-Levy et al. 2001; Polanyi 1978, 2001; Zelizer 2010; Graeber 2012; Hann and Hart 2011).

Does this lack of curiosity on the part of some political scientists reflect taken-for-granted assumptions about what 'the economy' is? Many who support the formal neoclassical idea of 'the economy' as distinct from human life also argue it is an objectively determinable phenomenon. In essence, there is only one true version of 'the economy', discerned most accurately by the experts, neoclassical economists themselves (Caplan 2001, 2008). The corollary to this approach may be a lack of open bottom-up research into plural understandings of 'the economy' because of an underlying assumption that people either understand the objectively determinable economy or they *lack* understanding of it, reflected in much work by economists on voters' folkloric or naïve beliefs (Caplan 2008; Leiser et al. 2010).

The economic relations and provisioning versions

In some political science fields, anthropology and economic sociology, there are two main alternative approaches to the formal approach, which I draw on at points in this book and briefly outline here.

The first emphasises 'economic relations'. Some political economists working from a more critical tradition argue that the formal understanding does not reflect how far 'the economy' depends on economic and social *relations* (Mitchell 1998, 2008a; Tooze 1998; Bourdieu 2002; Watson 2005, 2012, 2018). In essence, the impersonal forces are not so impersonal. They point to the framing of 'the market' as a thing particularly in the last four neoliberal decades (Crouch 2004; Watson 2018). Globalisation has contributed to an elite narrative of 'the economy' as beyond human control – as Bourdieu put it 'beyond contestation' (2002) – or depoliticised (Burnham 2001). 'The economy' is presented as having needs that are more important than social goals. This framing masks the extent to which 'the economy' is about people and how their social and political relationships are structured.

Some have argued there was always likely to be a backlash both against the rising economic inequality of the neoliberal decades and successive governments' depoliticising strategies. The backlash could take the form of rejection of the official version of 'the economy', or distrust in economic expertise, or both. For these political scholars, the backlash manifested in low-income people supporting Leave in 2016 because, despite thinking 'the economy' was important, they rejected the 'official version' of it spearheaded by politicians in the Remain campaign who epitomised a neoliberal and depoliticised approach that had not benefited them (Berry 2016; Colantone and Stanig 2016; Dorling 2016; Watson 2017).

The second, sometimes related, alternative to the formal version is an understanding of 'the economy' as 'provisioning'. Karl Polanyi (2001) pointed to the fact that the word 'economy' comes from the Ancient Greek for household economies: 'oikonomia'. Polanyi called such early and 'pre-capitalist' or 'pre-market' economies *substantivist* economies, because they were based on the idea that people needed to 'provision' for life and the way they provisioned was based on their social ties. In substantivist economies people relied on ideas about reciprocity, redistribution and social status, not just profit, and therefore 'the economy' was less distinct from social spheres of life than in the formal version.

Some feminist scholars argue provisioning more closely encompasses how women understand 'the economy'. More so than men, women's work is often unpaid and seen as outside the formal sphere. Feminist economists (Ferber and Nelson 2003) have drawn on the substantivist approach, as has Power in her understanding of 'the economy' as social provisioning (2004). She prefers the term 'social provisioning' to 'provisioning' to denote 'that at its root, economic activity involves the ways people organize themselves collectively to get a living' (2004:6).

Many who propose that we do see 'the economy' as provisioning, or would if the dominant framing of it was not as formal, are advocating for a more ideal kind of economy. Contemporary anthropologists Hann and Hart argue that 'the economy' should be seen as a *human* economy because 'in the end everyone should feel "at home" in a world that has been made by markets' (2011:170). Similarly to those political economists who believe there will be a backlash against neoliberalism, Polanyi (2001) believed that the neoclassical or formal approach was socially damaging. Followers of the 'formal' neoclassical approach claimed it was inevitable that when societies became 'market-based', their economies would become disembedded from social ties and that this was a natural and sustainable state of affairs. But Polanyi argued people will become desperate or angry enough to try to fight back, having what he called counter-movements against any economy that was 'disembedded' from society.

Those who see 'the economy' as in some way socially constructed (Berger and Luckmann 1971), rather than as an objectively determinable reality as neoclassical economists among others do, may be more open to the possibility that different people might have different understandings of it. This is the approach I have taken in this book. I did assume that understandings would vary in some way, but was open to what emerged from the field. I argue below that elements of all three of the understandings I have described here – the formal, economic relations and provisioning – emerged in various ways in participants' understandings of what 'the economy' means in Brexit Britain.

Asking directly

Before setting out the understandings that emerged from this fieldwork, I briefly describe the fieldwork and who the participants were.

My methodological approach is interpretivist ethnographic (Bevir and Rhodes 2015). Interpretivists argue that we should keep an open mind about what patterns in understanding, if any, might emerge. Therefore I decided to recruit participants from the fullest possible range of backgrounds. I interviewed people from age 18 to 80, spread roughly equally over the decades, and equal numbers of men and women. I interviewed them in two districts with contrasting income levels to make sure I talked to people in a range of economic circumstances. One district, where Diane and Misha lived, was to the north of the city's university and I gave it the pseudonym 'Hill District' and the other, where Rachel lived, was to the south of the university, with the pseudonym 'Church District'. My participants numbered sixty, small enough that I could talk to them in some depth and large enough that if very dominant tends emerged they might be representative of something in the general population, at the least worthy of further ethnographic or larger-scale study.

I chose to conduct the research in one city with a population of around 250,000 on the south coast of England. There is often commentary about the marginalised or left-behind in northern parts of England or Scotland, Wales and Northern Ireland. However, those living in the Southeast are not all wealthy (Boswell et al. 2018). The city was a thriving port with industries. Older residents describe working on the docks valeting cars, for the tugboat companies and at large foundries and car factories. A large proportion of those employed now work in what are described as elementary jobs, in factories or warehouses and the large retail sector. The city has been hit hard by rising economic inequality and the decade of austerity, becoming more deprived so that now one third of its children grow up in poverty.

The city still has a stock of council housing but there are acute shortages and long waiting lists because many residents cannot afford the high private rents, let alone the property ladder. In the last twenty years the biggest change to the population has been people moving into it from other European countries; between the 2001 and 2011 censuses the 'other white' population increased by over 200 per cent, from 5,519 to 17,461. There are suburbs of the city people call 'little Poland' or 'Russia'. This city contains two universities. On the university-subsidised buses long-term residents look on with closed expressions at young and well-dressed students from all over the world. I chose this city to research in before the June 2016 referendum but it demonstrated how unusual it was compared with other southeastern cities by narrowly voting to Leave.

This study's research design is based on an ethnographic sensibility that I describe in Chapter 2. Many political scientists and political economists deduce why people voted the way they did from the data on economic conditions they face or the demographic features they have, but at some stage research that asks people directly what they *believe* about 'the economy' is also necessary. Ethnographic methods are likely to be more effective than surveys in advancing knowledge about the beliefs of those groups in society whose experiences are furthest away from most political scientists. Mckenzie argues in her ethnographic study of working-class Leave voters that studies like hers are necessary because most political scientists either do not understand working-class narratives or misrepresent them (2017).

There is a particular need for ethnographic research into understandings of 'the economy' because it is such a nebulous concept. Many people struggle to put into words what they think 'the economy' means. Someone can use their everyday sense of justice to extrapolate to justice in the more abstract sense because at all levels justice is about the human realm. But 'the economy' is a more dualistic concept than society or justice. People I talked to were conscious that while they felt highly emotional about their personal economies, which were very much in their human domain, affecting things like their emotional relationships profoundly, they could not so easily translate these feelings to the abstract level of 'the economy'. Therefore, whenever I asked the direct question 'how do you define the economy?' I got thin responses along the lines of 'to do with money' and usually not much more (see also Norrish 2017). In the fieldwork for this book I got people talking in greater depth about 'the economy' by asking about their economic life stories and about features of 'the economy' they might have experience of, such as employment and debt, as well as the general term 'the economy' itself.

The participants' 'formal' and 'rigged' versions

I set out to research from the bottom up, open to the possibility that I might find lots of understandings of 'the economy'. I simplify what the following chapters reveal to be complex, but the core conclusion I drew from the fieldwork was that the understanding of participants in the low-income district was different to that of those in the high-income district. High-income participants seem to share the formal neoclassical understanding of 'the economy'. However, lower-income participants understand 'the economy' in a way that does not fit with either the formal or provisioning version, but is arguably close to the 'economic relations' one. The overwhelming sense of 'the economy' they have is that it is rigged by the rich. Perhaps surprisingly, people from each district shared an understanding regardless of which parties and economic policies, or sides in the referendum, they went on to vote for. As Cramer observes, people see 'the economy' though the lenses of their own experiences of it (2016:chapter 1).

I started interviews with economic life stories and people's experiences of employment. Employment and provisioning are characterised as 'struggle' in the lower-income Hill District and 'comfort' in the higher-income Church District. Hill District participants have been forced to adapt to the changing employment environments in ways that those in Church District have not.

In the higher-income Church District, people understand 'the economy', as the formal neoclassicals do, to be a broad umbrella term for impersonal forces that have the potential to benefit. They use the terms 'economy' and 'economic' often and with ease and a sense of familiarity. They sometimes talk about '*our* economy', as if they feel they belong to it and it is benign. For them 'the economy' is an umbrella, and a large one encapsulating many different aspects; prices, trade, employment, interest rates and exchange rates interact with each other and they see their own provisioning as connecting with the 'the economy' at many points. They have self-interest in following it closely, as Rachel does, to speculate in shares or anticipate mortgage rates. They recognise the potential for 'the economy' to be a positive force.

In contrast, for low-income participants such as Diane and Misha, everyday economies are intense struggles. The official economy affects their employment and living conditions in powerful ways but there are other aspects of the official economy, such as shares or even baseline interest rates, which they believe do not affect them directly. Therefore, they do not feel strongly connected to 'the economy' as a whole and the conception of it as an umbrella for forces that interact with each other does not resonate.

Many of the low-income participants in this book express little interest in following 'the economy' closely and may even believe following it will threaten their emotional wellbeing. They are more reluctant to use the term 'the economy' in talk about 'the economy', reflecting greater unease with how it is used in the official discourse. They do not share the sense of '*the economy*' as an impersonal phenomenon distinct from the human, because they believe powerful interest groups, often characterised as 'the rich', control it; 30-year-old Misha is one of many who say something along the lines of 'the rich write the rules'. I asked about underlying aspects of 'the economy' like austerity and the EU referendum issue of migration. Low-income participants are bitter about how rigged austerity was, how disproportionately it hit them. On migration, many see the lack of economic research into or politicians' concern about the localised effects of migration on their wages, their employment contracts or their social housing as a form of rigging by economic experts. These experts claim there will be benefits from migration to the 'overall' economy but those benefits never seem to trickle down to them. I suggest low-income participants may dissociate themselves[3] from the official version of 'the economy' in part because of what they see as the experts' lack of willingness to conduct localised research on the effects of migration.

Where does 'the economy' begin and end?

If participants contest what the term 'the economy' means, what else does this suggest? In talk about 'the economy' they also reveal something of where 'the economy' begins and ends for them and how it begins and ends in different ways for different people. This fieldwork raises questions about how political scientists categorise, and whether and how political scientists do it fits with how ordinary people do. I briefly outline three issues here that I expand on in later chapters. First, how should we approach categorising what is economic or non-economic? Second, is 'the economy' important to people? Third, are understandings of 'the economy' changing?

---

[3] Also see Lisa Mckenzie (2017) for an analysis of working-class Leave voters' 'dissociation' from the Remain campaign talk about the economy.

Entwining

Many scholars researching understandings mention forms of 'entwining'. Neoclassical economists believe people should not bring their moral or cultural beliefs into their economic reasoning – in effect should *not* entwine them (Caplan 2001, 2002). The only question that should be in someone's mind when deciding how to act economically or which politicians' economic policies they should support is 'will it achieve efficiency?' (Haferkamp et al. 2009). If they vote for efficiency they are more likely to achieve a cultural goal like fairness because everyone will prosper, whereas if they try to pursue fairness rather than efficiency, they will not get either. Economists despair that many people do in fact bring moral or cultural beliefs in to their economic and political reasoning, and they have survey evidence that those of lower income and the less educated do it more (Bazerman et al. 2001; Blinder and Krueger 2004; Leiser et al. 2010; Gangl et al. 2012).

Political economists writing on austerity have also claimed moral and economic 'entwining' occurs. I outline what they say about entwining to make a general point about categorising. Blyth (2013) and Gamble (2013) argued that, at the height of 'austerity acceptance' most people found personal debt morally repugnant, which made them susceptible to seeing government debt as morally repugnant and therefore a serious economic concern. The public had a dominant common sense that entwined their moral feelings about debt with their economic reasoning about government debt and the need to reduce it. Some political ethnographers also argue there is some entwining of economic and moral reasoning. One of the most illuminating ethnographies from the bottom up of beliefs about 'the economy' in the area of redistribution is Katherine Cramer's study of what the voters of rural Wisconsin believe about state funding programmes (2016). Cramer's starting puzzle is the question: why do people in Wisconsin (and elsewhere in the USA) increasingly vote against state spending plans, even when they might directly benefit from them? She notes this tendency is stronger in rural areas than in cities. She believes what emerges supports social identity theory – that people identify with a group, rural residents, and are suspicious or resentful of another group, urban residents, in part 'othering' them all, but in part othering them because aside from being urban they are also more likely to be black or minority ethnic. However she takes issue with those political scholars like Thomas Frank (2007) who explain rural America's rightward shift solely in terms of people becoming more attached to their cultural and religious values. She says this misses the point that both economic and cultural values are involved; rural residents 'intertwine economic considerations with social and cultural considerations in the interpretations of the world they make with one another' in a 'politics of resentment' (2016:7).

I ask, does everyone tend to 'intertwine'? Cramer chooses to study the rural areas only, vast as they are in a state like Wisconsin, so we do not see whether the urban residents also entwine their moral and economic reasoning in this way. I have argued that lower-income participants in this research see 'the economy' as rigged by rich people rather than impersonal, which might at first glance indicate that they are bringing their cultural reasons in more than higher-income participants. However, on the whole, contrary to the economists' studies I mentioned earlier, lower-income participants in this study do not bring cultural reasoning in more than higher-income participants. In talk about other issues such as debt, higher-income participants generally were more moralistic than lower-income participants. Higher-income participants, including Remainers, are as conflicted about 'how economic' their vote was in the EU referendum as lower-income participants suggesting the contrasting word clouds were always a simplification and that 'entwining' may be happening for people from all social backgrounds.

Categorising

This book raises questions about how people categorise what is economic from what is not. Economic anthropologist Graeber says we have to look at the moral and social bases of concepts such as debt, so central to the modern economy, and the central aim of his book is to investigate the 'moral basis of economic life' (2012:13). Cultural political economists Best and Paterson argue it is necessary to accept political economic phenomena as potentially having a cultural dimension due to their human element. However, they admit, such categorising is a complex business. Once scholars start to attempt it they may find how they categorise one sphere, such as economic, may then impact on how they define another (2010:21). This book does not contribute to theoretical discussion about categories, but, by describing everyday actors' understandings, it does at least increase the pressure on political scientists to be consistent in the application of categories.

For instance, is there consistency in the categorisation of opposition to migration? While the political economists I mentioned who still see 'the economy' as important tend to assume at least some of the opposition to migration is economic, some political scientists have argued that it should be seen primarily as a 'cultural' phenomenon. Inglehart and Norris are key theorists in this debate who I argue underplay the importance of economic drivers of opposition to migration. They adopt the Chapel Hill Expert Survey 2014 approach of categorising political parties that are 'against immigration' as demonstrating cultural rather than economic values (2016:32) and, even when they do ask specifically whether immigration is good or bad for a country's economy, code answers to that question as a cultural rather than economic attitude (2016:45). In Chapter 5 I expand on how participants in this study understand opposition to immigration to be more economic than Inglehart and Norris suggest. I raise the question: is there an element of being too influenced by the neoclassical economists' consensus that migration benefits 'the economy'? When people dispute that line of economic reasoning, arguing that they believe migration damages 'the economy', or at least some aspects of it, are some political scientists re-categorising what they would see as economic arguments as cultural arguments simply because they are the 'wrong kind' of economic arguments?

Relatedly, how should 'distrust' of expertise be categorised? Distrust is a dominant theme running throughout this book. The fieldwork in this book does support much other evidence that distrust cannot be categorised as primarily cultural, also having an 'economic' element.

Importance and changing understandings

At the start of this chapter I mentioned how prominent the debate about the importance of 'the economy' is. Do the understandings I describe throughout this book shed any light? First, because this book is about getting people to talk about 'the economy' in natural settings using their own words, it does enhance knowledge about the ways in which 'the economy' is important to people. I argue the fieldwork suggests 'the economy' is important to people whatever their income level, but that it means different things to different people.

Second, many scholars suggest that understandings of 'the economy' are changing and that this is due in part to the nature of 'the economy' itself during the neoliberal decades. It is hard to judge whether understandings of the term 'the economy' or how people might be entwining are changing, in part because there are few comparable ethnographic studies of this in past years to draw on. However, the strength of the sense of 'the economy' as rigged in the fieldwork for this book does indicate some greater degree of contestation compared with the past. The fieldwork also suggests that underlying understandings of 'the economy' are slow to change. At the start of interviewing in July 2016, whether Leave or Remain, participants were in a state of shock about the referendum result. From then until the final interviews in May 2018 the EU referendum was by far the dominant political issue, with other peripheral strands coming and going, such as winter NHS crises. Perhaps surprisingly, there was not much movement between 2016 and 2018 in beliefs about 'the economy' in relation to the European Union. The strong Leave interviewees in July 2016 were still adamantly Leave in the September 2017 focus group. There was more movement in belief in one of the other focus groups but it was by non-voters (from a pro-Leave to a pro-Remain position), so maybe they felt more able to change. On Brexit-related economic issues, despite media mention of trade, for instance, going from the level of superficial during the referendum campaign to acres of intense coverage of in-depth negotiations by 2018, participants' underlying understanding of that economic issue was not much affected by the passage of that time. This book is about understandings of 'the economy' in a time that is dominated by Brexit, but the underlying understanding seemed to have its roots in other past key events and watersheds, like 2008 as a harbinger of debt and austerity or 'the Thatcher years' in the minds of those aged sixty and over.

The findings in this book support much of the work of those political economists who argue the effects of the neoliberal decades and rising inequality were likely to change underlying understandings of 'the economy' so that people now see it as less benign, having less of a potential to benefit them than before. It also suggests that such underlying understanding as we apparently have in Brexit Britain may have been developing and changing for some time.

Plan of the book

In Chapter 2 I expand on the interpretivist ethnographic methods I use. I also introduce the districts and the participants in this study. For readers interested in greater depth on ethnographic methods I provide more detail in the Appendix. I explain how the interviews contain questions asking people about their 'economic life stories' and, to help get round the 'nebulous' nature of 'the economy', some questions on aspects of it, such as understandings of employment, debt, government spending, taxation, inflation, banking, trade and the economic effects of migration.

The theme of Chapter 3 is 'employment', or what Polanyi called 'provisioning'. It explores how people in the two districts make a living and how central this is to understandings of 'the economy'. In the low-income Hill District, when people tell their economic life stories there is much talk of 'managing', insecurity and radical job changes. Work is hard. There is a range of beliefs about unemployment and a lot of personal experience of unemployment and the reality of the unemployment figures. In the high-income Church District, while younger participants feel insecure as they face the future, those over forty who have been professional feel 'secure' and 'comfortable'. In Church district there are more detached views about unemployment although, strikingly, there is also distrust of government employment figures.

Chapter 4 explores what participants understand about the related issues of personal and government debt, government spending and taxation encompassing beliefs about austerity. This chapter yields some initial insights into how participants entwine cultural and economic reasoning. It also raises questions about the claims that people are so lacking in understanding that they are attracted to simple ideas.

Chapter 5 explores the themes linked by their dominance in the referendum campaign and post-referendum 'negotiation' period, of trade and the economic effects of immigration. Participants' understanding of trade is 'sketchy'. I explore understandings of migration, starting by outlining two planks in the cultural thesis of scholars like Inglehart and Norris, that opposition to migration was the most important issue for Leave voters and that opposition to migration is a largely cultural phenomenon. I consider neoclassical economists' assumptions that migration is overwhelmingly positive for economies and how that thinking permeates some political scientists' work. From the fieldwork I reveal a complex picture of how 'economic' opposition to migration is. I explore beliefs about the effects of the largely EU-originating migration into the city on employment conditions, wage levels and other resources like social housing. In many political works, people who oppose migration are believed to fear the 'Other'. However, the concept of the 'Other' is more varied in this book, as I show in Chapter 5. For some people the others are the 'less educated', for some they are 'older' people and for some they are 'the experts'.

In Chapter 6 I tackle what participants understand by the term 'the economy' as a whole, drawing on both their thin answers to the question 'how do you define "the economy"?' and the sense they have given throughout the rest of their interviews or focus group talk. 'The economy' itself is a 'hollow' word according to one participant, and a divergence emerges between the low-income and high-income districts. I explore the parameters of trust of economic expertise.

Chapter 7 concludes. I argue that while factors like political beliefs, education, gender and age shape understandings of the official economy, income or economic experiences appear to shape them the most. It is likely that the gulf in understandings has widened in recent decades and 'the economy' is now a more contested term than it used to be.

In Chapter 8 I suggest these findings have implications for political behaviour studies because lower-income people may be more reluctant to label their political behaviour as 'economic' and they may approach survey questions using the word economy as if it is a given with a greater degree of dissonance than they did in the past. I develop the argument that some political behaviour writers may have mistakenly taken people's reluctance to use the term 'the economy' as a sign that they do not care about economic issues and their cultural beliefs have become relatively more important. The findings raise questions about how political scientists categorise what is economic and what is cultural or moral. In general much scholarship implies that low-income people bring moral or cultural considerations into their economic reasoning more than high-income groups do. Throughout this book there are as many instances of high-income participants bringing in cultural reasoning as of low-income participants. I suggest that many political scientists both exaggerate and unjustifiably 'problematise' low-income participants' cultural reasoning. Therefore, I make a case for ethnography that includes people from a cross-section of backgrounds, rather than exclusive reliance on 'sectoral' ethnography, which explores usually marginalised groups in isolation. When a subject is as taken-for-granted as 'the economy' appears to be, then reflection on what it means should be from all quarters.

2

Researching understandings of 'the economy'

I introduced some participants in Chapter 1. Diane and Misha came from one part of the city I call Hill district and Rachel from Church district. In this chapter I introduce the districts and describe the methods I used to conduct the fieldwork this book is based on. The approach to gathering knowledge I use is interpretivist and the methodology is to research with an ethnographic sensibility. For readers unfamiliar with ethnographic methods or wanting to read more, I have included additional detail about the methods in the Appendix. For readers not interested in methods, go straight to Chapter 3.

Gatekeepers and conversations over bins

I found sixty people to participate using a combination of gatekeepers and knocking on doors. The first gatekeeper, George, introduced me to several people in Hill district and I attended his tenants' association meetings. The second gatekeeper was the deputy principal of a post-sixteen college. I knew it would be hard to find eigthteen-year-olds just by knocking on doors, and she gave me permission to talk to a couple of tutor groups to ask for volunteers to take part.

I found the rest of the research participants by being in the area, in the cafes and on the streets, striking up conversations in some cases as people gardened or took out the dustbins, or by knocking on doors. I put flyers through doors in key streets in each district and then knocked on them a few days later.

One man let me interview him purely because he had once done work like this himself, and, as a lifelong member of the 'market researchers' masonic lodge', agreed to any requests on principle. He was unusual. Apart from sympathy for me, participants' motives for agreeing ranged from wanting the honorarium to wanting to express their views about how it really was to politicians and other elite actors. Persuading people who had never taken part in research interviews or focus groups before, and who were private or busy, was a hard part of the fieldwork, but the fact that I did recruit so many participants who had never taken part in any academic research before, and did represent a range of social backgrounds, is a key strength of this book.

Hill district

George is a seventy-year-old UKIP organiser who is in touch with many of his neighbours in a council-run block of flats for the over-fifties. He invites me to a tenants' meeting in the Hill district area of the city.

The tenants' meeting George invites me to in July 2016 is held in a 1970s-built, four-storey building on the edge of an older council estate. It is one of the hottest days of the year and some residents are in the communal garden, designed for people to talk and sit on benches. The meeting is in the lounge off the garden. There are seven or eight in the room and it is chaired by a charismatic and organised woman called Beverley. Before they start, they chat and joke about health and George mentions plans to change the bus route because they are in competition with the needs of students. They let me introduce my research and several agree times there and then to be interviewed, giving me the numbers of their flats.

Hill district is high up and has incredible views across the South and areas of wild common and woodland. From George's block a road links into a big council estate built in the inter-war period. There are generous-sized semi-detached houses with big gardens front and back, living rooms with big windows, plenty of space and sound structures. This council estate is livelier than George's road. People on the street shout out to each other. It used to have a functioning mixed shopping street that is now largely devoted to fast food for university students. Hill district has high proportions of social housing and people on low wages and benefits, and there is resentment that the area is being gentrified so that younger families are being forced out to outlying estates to make way for more student housing.

The degree to which participants in Hill district perceive themselves as local and connected to the district varies. Misha, thirty years old, born there and still connected despite having been forced to move to the outskirts of the district by high rents in the last year, has an awareness of the differences even within the estate. She says there are distinctions between different segments that outsiders might not be aware of, a 'higher' and 'lower' end to Hill district.

> I'm quite confident in my own skin so it allows me to be who I am in front of anybody and everybody, so I can go from the lower end of Hill district to say the higher end and still feel comfortable talking and engaging with people as I would anywhere. I feel like I get a great understanding of how people view people; some say 'oh no we don't like to go down that end of Hill district, no we don't like to do that!' compared with people who say back to them 'you're stuck up, rich bitch!'

Some participants remember their parents helping to clear the waste ground in the middle of the estate in the 1970s, to make a playground. However, others have not lived there for so long. Lidia, originally Polish, finds Hill district friendlier than the one she lived in before, where nobody stopped their van being burgled in the middle of the day, but still only knows one of her neighbours and is scared of some of the others. Lachlan is a high-income student who feels there are not enough other students in the area, although, given the gentrification, that is a matter of time. Mona and Azad have lived here nearly a decade but most of their friends are from the country they emigrated from, spread over the city.

As I outlined in Chapter 1, I wanted to include participants from a range of backgrounds and one way to do that was to recruit participants from two contrasting districts. The contrast in the districts I chose was mainly along income lines. There are always tough choices to make when designing research and I accept that a shortcoming of this study is that it does not explore in great depth how those from different ethnic minority backgrounds might understand 'the economy', which might have emerged had I chosen districts divided mainly along ethnic minority lines.

Hill district is a ward of about 14,000 residents, only a mile apart geographically from Church district. A few of the residents I interview are high-income, but overwhelmingly the residents of Hill district are lower-income than Church district. The difference between the two districts is illustrated by the figures on child poverty. Out of the city's sixteen wards, 37 per cent of Hill district's children live in poverty compared with 21 per cent of Church district's. Hill district falls within the second decile of 'most deprived' LSOAs[1] in the UK. In Hill district, income levels are lower, there are fewer people with university education and/or a 'professional' occupation and there are lower levels of owner occupation and higher levels of social housing than in Church district.

The official statistics underplay the differences between the two smaller neighbourhoods in each ward that I chose to focus on. Within Hill district, I chose a network of about five interconnecting streets, all in the more deprived section of the district. Within Church district I chose a neighbourhood, a couple of interlocking streets, which is one of the most affluent.

Like many ethnographers I anonymise the city and names of the districts to avoid making participants fear they may be identified. Lane's study was of 'Eastport' (1962) and Cramer studies 'rural Wisconsin' (2016) without naming the villages and small towns. I gave participants pseudonyms. I found most participants wanted anonymity. They were giving personal details of their economic life stories and also in some cases felt defensive that they 'did not know enough' about 'the economy'. Mary, for instance, was relaxed in the interview up until the point when I mentioned the 'national economy', when she said 'this is where you'll get the answer "ooh, I don't know, I don't know!"'

---

[1] LSOAs are Lower Layer Super Output Areas, geographic areas that are used by the Department for Communities and Local Government (DCLG) to measure deprivation.

The approach in this fieldwork was not to assume at the outset that various demographic features, whether gender or income, would dictate people's understanding of the term 'the economy'. However, because I thought it was important to involve people from a *range* of backgrounds, I do set out here what some of those demographic features were. In both districts, as I was knocking on doors, I inevitably found, for instance, that older people were either more likely to be in or to have the time to talk. If I had just knocked on doors and interviewed the first sixty people willing to be interviewed they would have been predominantly older men. So I was conscious of the need to adapt my approach, by aiming particularly to find women who would agree to take part or altering the age range on the invitation I put through doors.

Some demographic details for the thirty Hill district residents are in Table 2.1: gender, age, educational level, occupational group,[2] political affiliation and how they voted in the 2016 UK referendum. Some of the participants in the Hill district table, like Misha, have recently been forced out due to sale of council housing stock and rising rents. But their families and social networks are still in Hill district and they continue to identify it as their neighbourhood. The Hill district participants are roughly 50 per cent women and are spread across age groups. Most are renting social housing and occupied in unskilled or semi-skilled work. Very few have been to university and in fact, due to the changes in school leaving ages, several left even before the age of sixteen. At the end of each interview I asked who they usually voted for in general elections and how they voted in the referendum, although that last point had often already emerged.

Church district

Rachel, from Church district, is the twenty-seventh person I interview. It is a beautiful day in October. Church district may only be one mile away from Hill district but it is another world. It is a conservation area and has an old-fashioned, 'village'-style sign depicting a parent walking with their child, saying 'welcome to Church district'. The streets contain a couple of classical grey stone spired churches and lots of huge trees, chestnuts and beeches. Houses are mainly detached, owner-occupied, built from Edwardian times through to the 1950s. The houses in Rachel's street are double-fronted, each with a front door that usually has a stone porch, from which you can peer into the bay window on either side. The trees and gardens are well tended, the road is wide without much traffic and there are birds and a common at the end of the road.

Most people I interview own their homes and are professional. In Church district only five of the seventeen participants work in the private sector and there is

[2] SEC measure of occupation, A, B, C1, C2, D, E. See www.ukgeographics.co.uk/blog/social-grade-a-b-c1-c2-d-e for further details.

Table 2.1 The thirty Hill district participants

Pseudonym	Gender	Age (decades)	Educated until	Occupation	Political affiliation[1]	2016 referendum
Adam	M	30s	School	C2	Lib Dem	Remain
Amelia	F	20s	School	D	Don't know	Not eligible[2]
Andy	M	60s	Univ	C1	Lib Dem	Remain
Azad	M	30s	Some univ	D	Don't know	Leave
Beverley	F	60s	School	D	Cons	Leave
Chris	M	60s	School	E	Cons	Leave
Colin	M	60s	School	C2	Lib Dem	Remain
Diane	F	30s	School	D	Non-voter	Non-voter
Doug	M	60s	School	D	Non-voter	Non-voter
Elena	F	30s	School	D	Labour	Leave
Elliott	M	70s	School	C2	Non-voter	Leave
Frances	F	80s	Univ	B	Centre Left	Remain
Gary	M	40s	School	C2	Labour	Leave
George	M	70s	Univ	C2	UKIP	Leave
Glenn	M	60s	School	D	Labour	Leave
Jean	F	70s	School	D	Labour	Leave
Julie	F	60s	School	D	Labour	Leave
Lachlan	M	20s	Univ	B	Cons	Non-voter
Lidia	F	40s	School	C2	Labour	Remain
Linda	F	50s	School	E	Non-voter	Non-voter
Martha	F	40s	School	C1	Centre Left	Remain
Martin	M	50s	School	C1	Cons	Remain
Misha	F	30s	School	E	Non-voter	Non-voter
Mona	F	30s	School	D	Don't know	Leave
Rosa	F	40s	School	C2	Labour	Remain
Ruby	F	50s	School	C2	Lib Dem	Remain
Ross	M	30s	Univ	B	Centre Left	Remain
Shelley	F	50s	School	C2	Non-voter	Don't know
Steven	M	80s	School	D	Labour	Leave
Trevor	M	70s	School	D	Labour	Leave

[1] I asked 'who do you usually vote for?'
[2] Amelia is not a UK citizen.

a preponderance of university-educated people who have worked in either education or medicine.

Bereavement counsellor Rachel is one of many in Church district who describe their childhoods as 'professional' but 'frugal'. Like surprisingly many on that road, she has family links with the RAF; her father had been a pilot who moved around and then ended up teaching flying on the edge of the city. She says:

My parents were very much in the... still in the 1950s, I would say ... Although we had a nice house my parents didn't spend money, they're certainly not frivolous

people in any way, shape or form so everything was 'make do' … sort of, you
mustn't be a spendthrift, you need to be quite careful and sure … My father was
talking about a pension when I was still at school. And we were given savings
certificates when we were younger every birthday and we knew that was there not
to be touched.

Rachel's theme of a 'frugal' upbringing is echoed by many others over the age of
forty in Church district. Stephanie (in her fifties) says that as a child:

we knew that that we didn't have a new hall carpet, which was threadbare. And
I knew that was because money was tight, but my dad preferred to spend money
on myself and my brother, on our education.

Harry (in his fifties) echoes the theme of a frugal upbringing with his memory
of pocket money.

With things like pocket money … I was only given very small amounts. I was
given one penny for every year of my life, which wasn't decimalised (laughs), so
I didn't get very much. So I just tended to leave it and let it accumulate and take it
all out at once, to make it worthwhile. So I did have a great sense of money being
worth a lot.

Michael, now in his seventies, remembers his father. He was a bank manager but
did not earn a high salary and had a large family, so their lifestyle was 'thrifty'
and 'frugal'. He says:

We always had food on the table, and we always had clothes on our backs and shoes
on our feet. But there were a lot of hand-me-downs.

While many describe their childhoods as frugal, most who are over forty also recognise they have achieved financial security in part because they are professional
and got onto the property ladder early on. They now have considerable property-
based wealth. The seventeen Church district participants are listed in Table 2.2.

Participants from outside the districts

Before I settled on the two districts, I conducted five pilot interviews both to
refine my methods and to explore different areas of the city. One was on the
edge of Hill district (with Robert) and four (with Helen, Paul, Theresa and Milo)
on the edge of Church district. The other 'out-of-district' participants were
eighteen-year-olds from the local sixth-form college I mentioned earlier, which
was equidistant between Hill and Church district. The eight students from there
came from a range of occupational backgrounds, as Table 2.3 indicates.

A sample of sixty can never be 'representative' of the population in the way a
larger group might be. However, the participants in this study do come from a
range of backgrounds; 60 per cent of participants are from occupational groups

Table 2.2 The seventeen Church district participants

Pseudonym	Gender	Age (decades)	Educated until	Occupation	Political affiliation	2016 referendum
Alan	M	40s	Univ	B	Centre Right	Remain
Alice	F	80s	College	B	Don't know	Don't know
David	M	70s	Univ	B	Lib Dem	Remain
Fawad	M	40s	Univ	B	Labour	Remain
Gareth	M	40s	Univ	C2	Don't know	Remain
Harry	M	50s	College	B	Cons	Leave
James	M	70s	Univ	B	Cons	Leave
Jane	F	70s	Univ	B	Lib Dem	Remain
Johnny	M	30s	Univ	C2	Labour	Remain
Joseph	M	70s	Univ	B	Don't know	Remain
Mary	F	70s	School	B	Don't know	Don't know
Michael	M	70s	Univ	B	Centre Left	Remain
Peter	M	70s	Univ	A	Centre Left	Remain
Rachel	F	50s	Univ	B	Cons	Remain
Rebecca	F	50s	Univ	B	Cons	Remain
Richard	M	80s	Univ	B	Cons	Remain
Stephanie	F	50s	Univ	B	Cons	Leave

Table 2.3 The thirteen 'out-of-district' participants

Pseudonym	Gender	Age	Educated until	Occupation	Political affiliation	2016 referendum
Callum	M	18	School	C2	Not eligible[1]	Not eligible
Clare	F	18	School	D	Not eligible	Not eligible
Helen	F	40s	Univ	B	Green	Remain
Howard	M	18	School	C2	Not eligible	Not eligible
Lisa	F	18	School	C2	Not eligible	Not eligible
Lucas	M	18	School	C1	Not eligible	Not eligible
Lucie	F	18	School	B	Not eligible	Not eligible
Maxine	F	18	School	E	Not eligible	Not eligible
Milo	M	20s	Univ	B	Labour	Remain
Paul	M	50s	Univ	B	Labour	Remain
Phoebe	F	18	School	B	Not eligible	Not eligible
Robert	M	50s	School	C1	Labour	Remain
Theresa	F	50s	College	B	Cons	Remain

[1] The eight students in this table were just too young to vote in either the referendum or the preceding general election.

C, D and E overall and it is significant that seventeen of the sixty are from occupational groups D and E, reflecting their proportion of the local population but also a marginalised group. Forty-eight per cent of the sixty participants are women. On national backgrounds, two Polish people agreed to take part and, where relevant, I refer to this when presenting their beliefs. Seven participants were from black and ethnic minority backgrounds. On age, particularly because of the involvement of eight eighteen-year-olds, the eventual spread was a reasonable one.

There is not such a balance with political affiliation. In the 2016 referendum, only sixteen of the sixty declared they had voted to Leave, although a couple more said they supported Leave. Of those eligible to vote in the referendum, three would not tell me how they voted and five were either non-voters, had not registered or had been ill. It is important to capture the views of those who do not vote – turnout at the referendum was high by previous standards but still only 72 per cent of those registered. Participants were less keen to say how they usually voted in general elections than to declare their referendum vote. Six were 'don't knows' or 'wouldn't says' and the number of non-voters who were too disgusted with politics to take part rose from five to six when it came to general elections. Hobolt et al. (2018) have recently argued that the referendum vote now represents a deeper cleavage than political party affiliation. Of those participants who were prepared to commit to a party affiliation, at least at the last election, there was a reasonable balance with fourteen Labour, twelve Conservative or UKIP and thirteen describing themselves as 'centrist' or Liberal Democrat.

Interpretivist approach

Interpretivists argue that what people believe is important because beliefs explain why people act the way they do (Bevir and Rhodes 2015:18). They question methods of research that 'read off' what people believe from their demographic features or economic conditions. Evidence that, for instance, voters in areas with low wage growth since the 1990s were more likely to vote Leave may be relevant (Bell 2016), but we also need to make the effort to ask people directly why they voted Leave. Interpretivists consider that research where people speak more openly on a subject using their own words complements surveys and enhances knowledge.

Research that predefines categories can sometimes be prescriptive. Beliefs people have on the subject of 'the economy' are likely to connect with other webs of belief such as on politics or society. Therefore, wherever possible, research design and the style of observation or questioning needs to be holistic, allowing participants to range freely, so that where they think their moral or cultural beliefs are relevant, they can express them. This has the benefit of helping to reveal how they delineate the economic from the non-economic.

Interviews and focus groups

Interviews

This is not ethnography in the full sense of lengthy immersion in people's lives (Rhodes 2017:43–4). I did not have the time to do a full immersion study where I was just observing. Immersive studies like the ones anthropologist Polanyi did with his team of researchers (1978) might have provided insights into how people understood their own economies, but the number of times they spontaneously broke into talk about politicians would have have been few and far between. Therefore, while there is some field notes-based observation in this study – of tenants meetings, shops and street corners – the core of the research is interview- and focus group-based. The research is therefore not fully ethnographic but it is conducted with an *ethnographic sensibility* (Pader 2006). Ethnographic sensibility encompasses

- critical awareness on the part of the researcher of what they bring to the field, their beliefs and predispositions and how that might be affecting the research process
- 'respect for differences of opinion and of belief systems' (Pader 2006)
- a 'profound ability to listen' (Pader 2006) and linked skills in asking questions and being able to analyse what people say they understand (Crewe 2015)
- interviewing as far as possible in everyday settings like homes

Forty of the sixty interviews were in participants' homes. I was exploring how people understood 'the economy' when they were trying to weigh up how to vote: engaged in activities like watching TV, going online, talking to friends and family. I needed to conduct the research in the place where people felt most free to express what they 'take for granted' (Pader 2006). Their homes were also the centres of their everyday economic lives, what they went out to work to maintain. When I interviewed inside people's homes I gained great insights. For instance, I was struck by how many formal dining rooms there were in Church district in a field diary extract I wrote after interviewing Joseph.

> House is not heated even though October and he seems frugal, quite smartly dressed, glasses, eyes very open and green. House tidy but slightly fusty smelling, like there are not enough people living there. There had been seven at one point he says and after his children left he'd taken in student lodgers, but obviously feels too old for that now. House is double-fronted detached, twenties style (like others in that road). He shows me into the dining room (yet again). We sit next to each other. Brown dark wood table with four chairs. Upright piano behind us with lots of children's photos. One arm chair in the room has lots of stuffed toys – for when grandchildren visit? Décor throughout is quite colourful. He is warm and friendly, has a sense of humour, very quiet voice. Very upset about the referendum result, says it made him feel sick. He asks me to stay for a cup of tea.

The interview design was semi-structured. In Chapter 1 I suggested it is difficult to research such a complex and nebulous phenomenon as 'the economy'. It might be possible to get one-sentence 'definitions' of 'the economy' as 'to do with money' but no more. Therefore my strategy was to divide interviews into three main sections: first, participants' economic life histories, second, their understandings of concrete features of 'the economy' and third, their understanding of the term itself. Each interview lasted about an hour.

ECONOMIC LIFE STORIES

Shelley, well-dressed in her early fifties, her back very straight because she has arthritis in her neck, pushes her granddaughter backwards and forwards in the pushchair to try to get her to sleep. She tells me I can start asking questions. My first question is 'what job were your parents doing at the point when you were born?' And, because she has to explain that her mother never worked for long because she was a manic depressive and often could not even get out of bed, Shelley or her father having to stay with her and her father having to work very long hours at night and Shelley sometimes having days off school, she opens the door to the kitchen and asks the women in there to push the child to sleep. She needs to concentrate on the interview.

Asking participants about their economic life stories can be personal and painful but it makes people feel at their ease in the sense that this is a subject they are expert in and can talk freely about. I often started with a factual first question, 'what job were your parents doing at the point when you were born?', like the one I asked Shelly. Participants sometimes needed a lot of prompt questions but sometimes, as in her case, it just started a narrative that she ran with. The 'economic life stories' sections of the fieldwork are interwoven throughout this book and could have amounted to a book in their own right. While participants told them fairly naturally, they also, at the end of it, often said that they had not done it often and that they found it interesting to do.

UNDERSTANDINGS OF FEATURES OF 'THE ECONOMY'

Economic psychologists Williamson and Wearing (1996) argue that one way to get round how nebulous and technical people often find the concept of 'the economy' is to also ask about more concrete aspects of it that they are likely to be familiar with. This approach is common in research on what 'representations' people have of technical or complex subjects, whether 'the economy' or genetic modification (Moscovici 1988; Roland-Levy et al. 2001). The problem is, *which* aspects of 'the economy' are people most familiar with? The choice of features might steer people in a certain direction in terms of expressing their understanding of 'the economy' overall. I chose not to include unpaid caring, which feminist scholars argue we should ask about. I chose not to ask about housing or health, even though

I found that some participants did subsequently talk about housing and health in the course of the interviews. My approach was to choose eight features of 'the economy' that are common in politicians' and media talk: taxation, government spending, debt, employment, banking, inflation, economic effects of migration and trade. I did also ask participants if there were any other features they thought should be added and used focus groups to explore this further.

Participants' understanding of the eight aspects chosen did act as a useful device to encourage people to talk about and build up a picture of their understanding of 'the economy' as a whole. However, another consideration is how to phrase questions. Many political scientists have documented that people often have not thought about what they believe on certain issues (Campbell and Converse 1960; Lane 1962). They can feel put on the spot when political scientists ask them and may search for recent media messages or other cues that do not reflect what they believe. Starting the interview by trying to emphasise that there was no such thing as a wrong answer and that it was about anything at all they thought they *knew or understood* about a feature produced a less defensive response than questions starting with 'what do you *believe* about...?' Therefore, after trial and error as part of an 'abductive' process of learning from the field-work, the eventual wording of the questions I fixed on for the second stage of the interviews was as follows.

- What do you understand about taxation?
- What do you understand about government spending?
- What do you understand about debt?
- What do you understand about employment?
- What do you understand about inflation?
- What do you understand about banking?
- What do you understand about the economic arguments about migration?
- What do you understand about trade?

In the rest of the interview I asked participants how they voted in the EU referendum and in general elections, what their understanding was of the term 'the economy' and how 'economic' they thought their recent political behaviour was. The interviews were semi-structured, with follow-up questions and questions sometimes asked in different orders. A full copy of the interview guide is in the Appendix.

Focus groups

I used focus groups to explore further what emerged from interviews. Agar and Macdonald (1995) iterate the advantage of running focus groups *after* interviews. Talk in interviews built up what they called frames of interpretation – in the case of their research, by teenage LSD users. They then explored these frames further in the focus groups and found some of them were confirmed and some thrown into question. They might not have been able to make sense of the focus group talk if they had not done the interviews first. I also wanted to gain deeper comparative insights in focus groups by inviting people I had already interviewed rather than new sets of participants.

Compared with an interview, focus group participants talk with one another, thus revealing shared understanding. I include many key focus group exchanges in the following chapters, which were unmediated and flow as conversations, notably on 'the rich' (see Chapter 6). There were three focus groups, one from Church district and two from Hill district. The focus groups focused on 'the economy' as a whole. I present insights from the focus groups interwoven throughout the findings chapters. Further details are available in the Appendix.

Timing

The interviews started in July 2016, the three focus groups were conducted towards the end of 2017 and the final interviews were conducted in May 2018.

Interpreting

How did I interpret the interviews and focus groups? I analysed transcripts using thematic analysis (Braun and Clarke 2006, 2013). To make that process come alive and in the interests of transparency about methods, I include here some extracts from transcripts on the subject of personal debt.

First, Chris, in his sixties and on disability benefits, described recent serious indebtedness due to non-payment of benefits.

> And [debt is] horrible [turns to wife], isn't it? People knock on the door and say 'I'm the bailiff!' And we used to say, 'we're not getting no money at the moment, how can we pay?' And they used to go away and say 'alright we'll get back to you' or 'you've got to pay this'. I said 'how can I pay when I'm not getting any money? Until I get any money I can't pay nothing'. I said, 'we're struggling'. I said, 'look in the food cupboard'. I said, 'it's empty'.

Diane, in her thirties, was on the minimum wage and still trying to pay off the debt from negative equity following the forced sale of her house post the 2008 crisis.

> I wouldn't go back that way [taking out a mortgage] … I just take every day as it comes now after what we've been through, that black hole [laughs] … It was out of our control.

In her late teens, Elena inherited her parents' debts and council house as well as having to become the carer for her younger siblings.

They were [payday loans], yeah, they were. Gas and electric, there was rent arrears that we had, credit cards were coming our way [laughs] ... yeah, there was just so much, oh catalogues and everything. Yes that's right, Littlewoods was another one. There was everything, just literally bombarding us. Definitely, it was horrible.

In her fifties and on benefits, Linda had taken out many payday loans and said:

I've been trapped in it for years and years and years.

Mary, now in her seventies and comfortably off, remembered the only time that she and her husband had been overdrawn, by a few pounds, and how disturbed they were by it.

No, that was the most debt we ever had, twelve pounds, but I remember that we did worry about it.

Analysing such rich and varied talk is difficult. The process of thematic analysis involves six systematic and lengthy stages of coding and developing themes, which I outline in the Appendix. I started by reading and coding all sixty interviews (and later focus groups) for beliefs about personal debt *in alphabetical order* so that I was not assuming a pattern based on the districts or any other factor. I then grouped codes under the headings of themes. Two overarching themes emerged on personal debt: one of 'personal debt is to be feared' and the other of 'personal debt is to be avoided'. All of the extracts quoted above seemed to fit the 'to be feared' theme except Mary's, which fitted more closely to 'debt is to be avoided'. Overwhelmingly, those from Hill district fitted the first and those from Church district the second theme, so when I wrote up the analysis of debt I divided it into the two districts. I did find that a pattern often, but not always, emerged, where Hill district participants tended to fit with one theme while Church district ones fitted with another.

Unlike surveys, where another researcher should be able to replicate the same findings, in ethnographic research the researcher has to be clear what standards they are using to ensure the research reflects as accurately as possible what participants said. In this study I have attempted to meet three standards. First, I have attempted throughout to keep my own predispositions out of the way I either conduct the research or analyse it, not a choice all ethnographic researchers make. I took this approach because I was trying to recruit participants who might never have participated in academic research, without in most cases an introduction from a gatekeeper, and thought it would be most reassuring to present myself as a researcher who just wanted to record their views in non-judgemental mode. Once the interview started, I did sometimes break the ice by sharing details of my history, but I never got the impression that participants were interested in hearing a lot about what I thought. Instead, they did see me as a vehicle for reporting their views.

Despite attempting to present myself as a 'neutral' researcher, I accept I cannot keep my beliefs out of this research process completely. I am not objective and therefore that I also need to reflect critically at every juncture (Schwartz-Shea and Yanow 2012). As someone who is opposed to racism, for instance, I did not want to show that opposition in interviews because I did not want to look as if I was judging and I wanted participants to feel they could speak freely. However, I usually left the interview to write up how it had made me feel in my field diary in the hope that such a process of reflection would mean I could analyse and interpret such views as accurately as possible. I do not want to give the impression that the only issue for critical reflexivity was my being disturbed by racism. There were other issues. I was also aware that I came from a high-income and educated background, and had to avoid making assumptions or being condescending. I was often unsettled that I did not feel I fitted with the high-income participants either. For instance, I had not had the frugal tradition that many of them had reported their parents passing down to them.

I aimed to be critically reflective, but not allow my recognition of my positionality to detract from the purpose of faithfully interpreting participants' beliefs in as accurate a way as possible. Rhodes is right to warn that the danger of too heavy an emphasis on critical reflectiveness will both stop us making efforts to 'see clearly' and squeeze out the participants' voices.

> Critical self-awareness is essential but the danger is that the text becomes about the researcher; a diary of his or her involvement in the field. An excess of reflexivity spills over into the narcissism that is as unpalatable as it is boring ... The goal of remaining a 'professional stranger' balancing engagement, detachment and critical self-awareness is equivalent to searching for the Holy Grail – always out of reach. Yet, there is no alternative to trying – it's life as we know it. (2017:52)

Second, I have tried to be accurate about how prevalent beliefs were. I include many direct quotes from participants and choose to include a large proportion of quotes with fewer of my words interpreting, rather than a smaller number of quotes analysed in great depth using my words. I try to quote from the full range of participants. Relatedly, I use numbers more than some ethnographers. They believe frequency is not the same as saliency or that the use of numbers is less appropriate in qualitative research, given participants have not been asked exactly the same questions (Braun and Clarke 2013:261). However, I follow Sandelowski (2001); *where appropriate* it may be more transparent to count. The reader knows the context and research design so can judge validity or relevance for themselves. Therefore, I use terms like 'most' when there was more than half, 'some' when it was more like half and 'few' more like one quarter, and I also do sometimes count and give an exact number.

Interpretivist ethnography aims for 'complex specificity in context' (Rhodes 2016:211) that edifies (Rhodes 2017:50). My task is to persuade others that the complex specificity in context has been developed in such a rigorous way that it does edify. Therefore I argue that I can generalise from the findings, in the idiographic sense that if there is a dominant theme in a small study, this points to the possibility of its existence at the population level, particularly if the theme emerges strongly from the context, which large-scale surveys may miss (Sandelowski 2004:1380).

Conclusion

The focus of this book is the understandings of participants rather than the use of ethnographic methods. I assume there is no need to labour the point about the value of ethnographic methods. Most interpretivist ethnographers draw on the full range of evidence, whether surveys, evidence of conditions or ethnographic ones, and hope researchers from different perspectives will do the same. Sometimes, however, more positivistic or quantitative-based researchers are less reciprocal in taking note of ethnographic studies than we are in taking theirs into account. Rather than exhaustively explain methods, I have given an overview in this chapter and provide more detail in the Appendix. Previous researchers may have been put off from researching everyday understanding of 'the economy' in part because they believed it would be too difficult, but these interviews and focus groups generated full, rich and varied data.

3

Provisioning: 'whole buildings have disappeared'

Beverley, in her sixties, brings down some tea-making equipment to the lounge of her block of flats when it is time for me to interview her. She is open and talks fast and at great length. Her experience of semi-skilled employment patterns may strike chords with many other residents of the low-income Hill district. Beverley jokes about some of the grimmer aspects of her employment history.

> But it was so funny, I had been made redundant so many times I actually asked them if they could make me redundant; because they said 'we can't sack you', but they said 'we could make you redundant'. And I said, 'yes please!' [laughs]. It used to be a laugh, because when I saw any of my friends they used to say, 'please don't come work for us!' because not only was I made redundant, but whole buildings have disappeared.

Beverly was born in Hill district. At the point when she was born her mother was working as an usherette, later a cleaner, and her father was a bus driver, later working in the Merchant Navy. They inherited her grandmother's council house on the older estate next to where she now lives, and she describes relatives living in the streets around them and how at one stage they moved all their belongings in a wheelbarrow. She says:

> This sounds really ridiculous because you wouldn't [do] that nowadays, but they were taking the furniture from the old house to the new house, coming up and down the road with the wheelbarrow [laughs]. So you can see we didn't have washing machines or anything like that.

Beverley is matter-of-fact in remembering only one family holiday away, with only one photo taken of the children on the steps of a caravan. She left school at sixteen with the aim of training to be an audio-typist, but she had to downgrade to that of clerk typist. However, she loved her first job as typist in a factory until she was made redundant when the factory closed. Beverley had many other jobs, such as for a tug company in the docks and in shops, but mainly she worked as a telephonist. She was trained initially on the 'old-fashioned',[1] where you needed

---

[1] Incoming calls come to one central switchboard where a switchboard operator connects the call to the appropriate person by inserting a phone jack into their extension.

to be a certain height to be able to move the manual plugs around the connecting board. There are great embellished details in Beverley's story, such as that in the tug company her co-worker was full-time, but only worked part-time, 'because she was the fancy woman, she used to go out with the old boss'.

Beverley never earned a high wage and was at times a single parent with sole financial responsibility. She does not use the term 'working class' to describe herself. But when she talks about her childhood and parents she is open that they never had money, that her father was one of the first to exercise the 'right to buy' a council house towards the end of her childhood, but that even then it was always a struggle. She says she inherited a tradition from her parents of not getting into debt and of budgeting in a physical way. She describes how as a young adult:

> The council never paid your rent [direct], you know like they do now. You had your money and you had to sort it out. So I had seven tins, empty tins of Sun Valley tobacco, and I had gas, electric, rent – I had everything labelled on these seven tins.

Towards the end of her working life she experienced ill health such as osteoarthritis, which became apparent when she worked in a store and when she tried to re-train to be a hairdresser.

A common experience that emerges from her story, and that of all other Hill district participants with more than a couple of decades of employment history, is of deindustrialisation, forced occupation changes and increasingly temporary work, or 'precarity', as Standing describes it (2011).

Several of the male participants started out in factories or breweries doing stable, sometimes skilled, jobs and ended up driving lorries or cabs, often on an increasingly low-paid, self-employed basis. Elliott, now 76, experienced a drop in status and security of his employment conditions during his working life. He started in the Navy as a 'marine engineer', repairing and refitting engines, but when the shipyards started closing he switched to decommissioning in the nuclear industry, heavy work, handling the material in protective suits. He was made redundant from that due to technological change and was shaken by the unemployment he experienced afterwards.

> Unfortunately, from 1972 onwards I was in and out of work. One time I could pack in a job one day, walk to another company and get another job the same afternoon to restart the following morning. Well, those days are long gone. Obviously … when they retired me from the [nuclear plant], I thought I'd walk straight into a job, but I finished up having to go to an agency. Because I've still got my HGV and all of that heavy goods licence, that's the way I managed to keep in a job, working for somebody who was taking a percentage of my work. They were paying me but they would get a big percentage. I finished up working as the night operations manager for Y company, in their warehouse.

There are stories from older participants reflecting lack of educational opportunity. Colin, now in his sixties and a landscape gardener having worked in service, started off as an apprentice boilermaker.

> I wanted to go to Art College because I got CSEs and all that … in Art and I really wanted to do that, but my parents just couldn't afford it. So [my father] said 'go and get an apprenticeship, if you've got a skill you can go wherever you want'. And that's what I did. I went and got a skill, got an apprenticeship … The black arts as they say [laughs]. Plating. Boilermaker. You have to do everything. So it was very thorough you know, and you'd go from plumbing to plating and all sorts of things.

Younger participants, such as Gary in his forties, also experienced radical changes in jobs.

> I worked in foundries, metalworking, all industrial stuff really for about a year and a half, different companies. Then I started to settle a little bit, I can't remember the name of the company … and it was making parts for electrical motors. I was there for a couple of years … I did my forklift truck training … and then I worked … washing metal parts to get rid of the chemicals off things. You needed a forklift truck to empty things into it. Did that for a long time, then I had a breakup with my partner up there and moved down to here and I worked then on the docks … with the car companies. I first started with a valeting company cleaning brand-new cars that come through. It was all right; it was just the way the hours were, it was very strange hours. I thought 'I've had enough of this' [laughs] … and I started working in retail again.

As well as the factories and retail he has been in the armed forces and is now happy working in the health sector. In fact, whilst many of the Church district residents have experienced decades in the same job, such as university librarian or doctor, only two of the Hill district residents have: Jean, as nursing assistant for thirty six years, and Ross, one of the few-higher income Hill district residents, now in his forties, who has always worked as a teacher.

Employment is key to economic life histories and to what Polanyi (2001) called 'provisioning'. Employment affects participants' 'local' economies profoundly and is one way that the broader national economy can affect them. So in this chapter I focus on what participants say in their economic life stories and in direct response to the section of the interview where I start by asking 'what do you understand about employment?'

Hill district

'Managing'

Many Hill district participants have experienced childhoods where money was tight. Jean, now in her seventies, says they knew money was tight.

Because we had one pair of shoes for the winter, one pair of shoes for the summer and that's how it went on. When we sat to the table at teatime there was one loaf of bread and we used to have so many slices, and if it had all gone we couldn't have no more because she had no more money to buy it with. She did make cakes, my mother, to fill us up. We used to come home to dinner at dinnertime so we had a cooked-dinner dinnertime, so it was only teatime that we had it, yeah. Money was very, very tight. Some days my dad worked seven days a week for weeks on end.

Gary is decades younger than Jean, in his forties, but also experienced poverty in his childhood.

Gary: Very. [Money was] very tight.
Interviewer: Can you say a bit about how you used to notice that?
Gary: Umm lack of food, lack of treats, school shoes with paper in the bottom because we couldn't afford new shoes. So yeah, really tight, those sorts of things. Hand-me-down clothes, things like that. No electric, no gas, ice on the inside of the windows when you were a kid, so yeah.

Like Beverley, most participants over sixty in Hill district mention physical budgeting in the form of jars or tins for key bills. Few have been highly paid. Only a couple have been able to get on the property ladder.

A dominant theme is that Hill district participants speak of life as managing, survival and a day-to-day struggle. Analysing transcripts for the frequency with which some words are used confirms the dominance of the theme; a word frequency count using NVivo finds 115 references to 'survival', 'managing', 'getting through' in occupational groups C1, C2, D and E interviews but only 7 in those from occupational groups A and B. Diane, a cleaner and care assistant with children in her thirties, mentions 'struggle' or 'manage' several times.

Even eighteen-year-old low-income participants *expect* life to be a struggle: Callum at eighteen already says 'as long as I can manage okay ... I guess that's all I want' about his future life.[2] Elena, in her thirties, hopes her family is going to 'be able to bear' the future.

The struggle manifests in food in some cases. Rosa, in her forties, has had a lot of 'egg and chip dinners'. Shelley, in her fifties, eats beans on toast for days. Several of the older Hill district participants express pride that they have managed. One phrase echoed separately in interviews by a married couple and widower, all three in their seventies and eighties, epitomises 'life as struggle'. They say they are proud they 'got through life'. Jean says 'We managed, *we got through life* [laughs]. We still do manage now'.

I explore in more detail in Chapter 4 the belief that, given the difficulty of managing on tight incomes, many fear debt.

---

[2] Callum does not live in Hill district but in a similar area.

'Working to live'

Some say they feel work gives them status and self-respect and enjoy aspects of it. Elena says 'you lose yourself' without it; Lidia, in her forties, says she loves to feel as a health worker that she has made a difference. However, they both also perceive work as hard and needing mental and physical reserves to manage. Most in Hill district talk of how hard and grinding work can be. Lucas, aged eighteen,[3] talks of his father working such long shifts for low pay.

> [He was] coming back to go to sleep, wake up and then go early for work next day … just working to live.

Callum's[4] mother was working in a care home but the shifts were twelve hours; his father's work was getting more physically demanding as he got older. Jean found being a nursing assistant, a job she did for decades, physically demanding, dealing, for instance, with dementia patients and often requiring unpaid extras.

> It's hard work … very hard work.

Sometimes it is not just the physicality or monotony of work but social conditions like isolation or feeling degraded by lack of access to toilets that rankles, as Elena remembers of one job where she was in:

> this tiny little alcove. And I sold fruit and nuts and health foods and I was there for two years, but it was horrible because you always had to work alone and there was no toilet on site. It was horrible [laughs].

Some in their thirties and forties have had opportunities to re-skill and train for higher-paid work. Rosa, previously a factory worker, went on retraining courses provided by New Labour as a single parent. She then ran similar courses to encourage young women back to work and has also worked in Sure Start centres and schools. Gary now studies on top of a full-time job, but the stress of living on a low wage that means he and his partner never go out and combines with the demands of his younger children when he is trying to study. He says:

> It's been very stressful financially probably. Stressful where we're always staying in, that can be really hard. When I'm studying the girls say 'oh don't study today, play with us instead', and I sort of think it makes me feel guilty for studying. At the same time I say 'I've got to do this. If I don't do this we'll suffer a lot more in the end'.

Some in their thirties and forties worry there will be fewer training opportunities for their children. Rosa fears the effects of contraction of the initiatives

---

[3] Lucas does not live in Hill district but in a similar area.
[4] Callum does not live in Hill district but in a similar area.

she benefited from, which she believes will lead to 'social breakdown'. At the same time, some express anger that some courses still provided for the young, effectively the raising of the compulsory school leaving age, will keep unemployment figures down whilst not being high-quality enough to lead to secure jobs at the end. Linda is deeply pessimistic about the prospects for her grandchildren. She says poverty is already increasing and will continue to do so.

> It's so sad to know that my grandchildren are going to be them people.

'Carrot-and-stick' beliefs about employment

When I ask 'what do you understand about employment?' many mention increasing job insecurity, manifest in zero-hours contracts and 'self-employment'. Three themes emerge. First, that zero-hours contracts are unfair. George mentions a house down the road where several young single men are on them, and that it is 'not fair'.

> The quality of employment is bad. The people who employ a lot of these people probably bring up the employment figures but it's not really employment is it? It's not what I call employment. It makes the Tories look good.

The second theme is that zero-hours contracts render the worker powerless. For instance, Andy says they are:

> going back to the Victorian times. You know you stand at the door like down at the docks, 'we will have you for today and that's your lot'.

The third theme is that zero-hours or casualised contracts make people feel insecure, echoed in Gary's comments.

> They might work for some people but I would say the majority of people who are going for the jobs and are being put on these don't want a zero-hours contract. They want stability to be able to know exactly what they're getting every week and things like that.

Martin, working in a security firm, in his fifties, knows people who have been forced by the lack of regular employment to become 'self-employed' but:

> actually, when you dig down underneath, they're not making any money.

On low pay, Hill district participants use phrases like 'everybody's got bills but it doesn't cover them' (Colin, in his sixties). They often make a link between beliefs about low pay and unemployment. Martha and Glenn say the dividing line between unemployment and low-paid work is too narrow. This is reflected in one of the Hill district focus group exchanges.

Shelley: A lot of people who are trying to get into work, it's not beneficial if they get into work, because they don't earn enough money as they would on income support.

Misha: Job centre said to me, 'it will not benefit you to go into work'. She basically said to me 'don't go into the job – you'll be financially worse off'.

Shelley: People don't want to go to work for nothing.

Gary, who has always been in work, says, 'I hate the idea of unemployment. It just scares me.' There is criticism of the tougher benefits and signing-on regime. Colin and his wife were in domestic service as a couple. When she died suddenly, he faced unemployment in his fifties. He was computer-literate but, even so, the dehumanising nature of the new online system to register as job-seeking shocked him. He comments that being unemployed saps the confidence, perhaps particularly of the young.

> Every day I sat at that thing [computer] for hours and hours. It drives you mad. I sent off hundreds and hundreds of CVs and things like that. What annoys you, you don't even get a reply, you don't get a thanks, you know, and I think it's quite disconcerting. And that's for an older person, for a younger one it's even worse.

Colin mentions other obstacles, such as a lack of buses to distant job centres or the problems of those who do not have computer access. Glenn, in his early sixties, says:

> I'm unemployed. I was on ESA, now JSA.[5] I was unfit to work for physical reasons. I can now work, but the sort of work I've done previously I couldn't do. I think … thirty years ago I wouldn't really have been able even to think about what it really meant, but being unemployed now, I can understand it, and the exploitation of people in employment that sometimes happens. Sometimes people are better off unemployed than employed.

Some know people who are both 'too depressed' to work and too depressed to survive on benefits, and there is real concern about the benefit sanctions regime. Shelley, in her fifties, who volunteers in a food bank, says people need encouragement to get out of unemployment. She believes that all should work and it should not be easy to start on a road of claiming benefits. However, the current harsh sanctions approach to reducing welfare dependency will not help to achieve that goal.

> I think people get so down, they get so depressed because of the lifestyle. They need encouragement, they need courses to go on, encouragement, not just, say, 'go out and get a job or your money is stopped'. People just go down. I know. I do a bit of

[5] ESA is Employment and Support Allowance; JSA is Job Seeker's Allowance; both are names of benefits paid to the unemployed.

voluntary work with my church here and ... we give food bags out, and there's so many people who've been sanctioned because they never went for an interview or they've missed an interview. And they've had all the money stopped and they've got no food, they've got nothing. They've got to wait more than six weeks before the money gets started. They're really down people, they're really depressed, and they've got no encouragement to go out to work. I think if there was more encouragement and more like 'you can do this' instead of just 'your money is going to stop if you don't go out to work' ... People don't even care if their money's stopped; they just, they can't get out to work.

Rosa argues that there are only a tiny percentage fraudulently claiming and that the media 'scaremongers'.

You are only going to get those people stuck on benefits with no way out. So they took the way out and now they're punishing them for being stuck there, whereas with the Labour before, they invested a lot of money into dragging people out of that poverty situation into a re-education, retraining, finding new values, education in healthy eating. So now I'm feeling it's all stick and no carrot. Whereas the carrot was much more successful at encouraging people to change their ways, now, just stopping their money creates a bigger problem rather than the solution to their problems. So it's going to cost a lot more in the long run again.

However, some were brought up in families where accepting life on benefits was the norm and they have striven to work themselves. Elena, in her thirties, took on her parents' council house, their debts and care of her younger siblings. She now foster cares and depends on in-work benefits from her partner's job, but hopes his promotion will mean that is not necessary. Some are ambivalent about whether to criticise the unemployed. Misha, now in her thirties, was also brought up by parents on benefits and says:

So unemployment, at first I thought it was the greatest thing ever to get unemployment benefits; you could do whatever you want, you don't have to do nothing. And then, as I've got older, I feel like a lot more people are a lot lazier and I feel the government could be doing so much more to make people get into work.

Clare[6] is only eighteen but several members of her family are unemployed.

Unemployment. I know that it's very difficult. A lot of people in my family have the experience of unemployment. I've seen that through people. Like some of them don't make the effort, a few members of the family don't try and go out and do something about it, but it's devastating when you see the people that do actually try and they try a lot, and it's the same effect and they just don't get a job.

A few are more critical. Lidia disputes that there are no jobs.

---

[6] Clare does not live in Hill district but in a similar area.

I've been working all the time to be honest, and if somebody is unemployed I don't understand this, why? ... Like I said, if I could have a choice to work less I might just cut down my hours, but never be unemployed. I feel important when I'm working and when I go to work. I've been doing my work for a long time and the specific job I'm doing in the hospital, I know I'm doing it well. I've got a lot of good feedback from patients and other colleagues and that's making me feel important. So ... I know that there's a lot of unemployment in the area, our area as well, but this is something I can't see myself.

Diane says she notices mothers at the school gate, who she believes get pregnant again just as their oldest child reaches the age where government regulations would force them back into work.

Church district

Like the majority in Church district, Michael and Rachel went to grammar school. Fawad (in his forties) came from a poorer background than most other residents and is one of the only ones who went through the non-selective school system, then going into business rather than a profession, with a high income now. All except one Church district participant have a form of higher education.

'Never any doubt we would be secure'

In marked contrast with Hill district participants, twelve of the seventeen Church district participants have had the same careers throughout most of their adult lives. For instance, five have worked mostly in medicine, four in education. Even for those in the private sector, they have risen up career ladders within the same sector. David underwent lengthy medical training to become a consultant and says:

Oh yeah, there was never any doubt that we would be secure. And there was never any doubt that we would have enough to live on quite comfortably. There were no risks.

Michael chose the greater security of public-sector academic work over less-secure banking.

Solvency was very important to my father I think, and it was also important to me ... it suited me well temperamentally to be in a career where the job security was high and I'm conscious that, looking round today, if I'd gone into banking I would have made three times the salary. But I valued the lifestyle and that's the way it happened and my life worked out.

There were periods when Michael could not afford holidays but:

We've always been financially stable and I suppose from my point of view that's quite important ... So yes, we were extremely lucky.

Those Church district participants who work in the private sector feel less secure but value their work and believe they have the skills that will keep them employed at high wages. Alan comes from a less-secure background in that his small-business-owning parents at one stage went bankrupt, so he was conscious from an early age of the swings of fortune involved in business. He went to university and then straight into business rather than a more professional route, although it took him a while to settle in the property business. He now owns a property letting business, but despite it being in the private sector says 'I guess I feel reasonably secure'.

Older Church district participants often feel particularly conscious that they have experienced a security the younger generations will not. Joseph, retired teacher in his seventies, says:

I just feel sorry for young people these days, you know. I had such an easy ride really. My education was free, I walked out of university and I lined up six jobs.

Some younger high-income participants do fear future insecurity.

Realistically, so many people now are going to have five or six jobs in their lifetime it's not going to be one fixed thing ... it's going to be a really temporary environment which is, I'm not gonna say whether it's good or bad, but it's different, it's quite uncertain. (Phoebe, 18[7])

'Comfortable'

In an NVivo word frequency count of the interview transcripts there are twenty-six references to being comfortable or secure by participants from occupational groups A and B, but only six in those from occupational groups C, D or E. While some who perceive themselves as comfortable are still keen to be careful with their money, including assiduously learning about the best financial advice, others do not count their money as closely as in Hill district. Michael says 'I've got more interesting things to do in my life!'

Rachel and her partner have been able to retire early. Rachel believes it is important to be careful about money, using phrases like 'we've got to cut our cloth according to ...', but she also has enough of an income to be able to speculate in shares.

Retired engineer James says:

I've almost never worried. There have been times when we moved, well we moved several times, and one time when we moved before we went to X and then when we

7 Phoebe does not live in Church district but in a similar area.

moved back to UK, each time we sold houses. When we moved back and bought the house we're now in, it was a stretch, and there was a time actually after we'd been in a few months that actually we were wondering, well, 'are we going to be able to afford to do this?' But, well, we persevered and we survived and we had, I had, a reasonably good job with Y and we had a very good employee share scheme which actually worked out unbelievably well for us, it made a big difference to our financial situation. I can't believe how lucky we were actually to be in that place at that time and that was fortunate.

Most of the participants own their own houses, which have appreciated hugely in value. Michael says:

But you know ... with this house, we bought it in 1977 when we came here, five young children under the age of ten, not as some neighbours heard the rumour ten children under the age of five [laughs]. And if you remember in the 1970s, early 1980s when Mrs Thatcher became Prime Minister during the period of very high inflation, we lived through that and of course what I saw was ... my own salary in money numbers rocketing upwards. I've also seen in recent years the notional value of the house has gone up by twenty times ... In fact I think if I came here now ... I couldn't afford this house.

As with all Church district participants over fifty, he did not seem to have financial concerns in retirement. Alice, now in her eighties, who says 'we've always been pretty safe most of our lives', also feels comfortable during retirement.

I am completely ignorant. I couldn't tell you what my pension is except that I get two, old age and my teaching pension, and it's enough to keep me going each month ... No, we were both very protected, pension-wise ... My husband gets three.

Joseph says, 'my only financial worry now is how I can give as much as I can to my kids'.

'Tricky' beliefs about employment and unemployment

In response to the question 'what do you understand about employment?' Church district participants do not tend to mention problems with their own employment, but four mention the underemployment or precarity of employment for those on zero-hours contracts, coupled with at least a third mentioning problems of the low-paid.

I think the whole zero-hours culture is totally pernicious; it should never have been allowed. (Peter)

There is an increase in zero-hours contracts, which again is very concerning. (Harry)

I know that people are working long, long hours and can't keep a family on it and they're afraid of unemployment … if they don't jump they're out of the job, and it's not good. (Rachel)

I know [unemployment is] reasonably low at the moment although quite a lot of people have part-time jobs or have gone self-employed. (Gareth)

Stephanie worries that people work long hours and cannot pay bills.

Those in the private sector are concerned about skills shortages. Fawad is deeply concerned about the electrical engineering skills shortage, on a voluntary board to try to attract more graduates, upset that his own children have gone into finance rather than manufacturing, concerned at 'the more global competitive space', including China's huge numbers of graduates. He cites the example of his uncles in the Ford factory.

They worked there for twenty, twenty-five years and then cousins who started working there, they probably worked there for two or three years, then the whole thing closed and went to Turkey and Poland.

He argues for an industrial strategy, Jane for more 'active government' in this area. Peter, who has worked on mechanisation and automation, echoes concerns about the effect that has had and will have even more on employment in the future.

On unemployment, two-thirds have no direct personal knowledge of it and proffer that straightaway in their answers, often recognising they have had great security in their lifetimes. As Peter, retired executive in his seventies, says:

Unemployment is something I've never suffered, so I'm very lucky.

One third of Church district participants have had some personal experience. This latter group includes those who have been forced to give up or scale down work due to ill health and two of the younger interviewees. Johnny (in his thirties), who has been unemployed for some years, says 'there is no longer any stability in employment'.

There is only one explicit reference to the unemployed being work-shy.

I think there are a lot of people sitting on doorsteps of shops with a cap open, young people, who could probably go out there and get a job, I really do. (Alice)

Although Alan, an employer, is ambivalent about whether all unemployed people should be made to work because he says some of them are effectively 'unemployable'.

You know, if somebody said to you, 'look, you can have this person to work for you free, the government will pay for them to come here', you'd say, 'I'd really rather not have that, because they are a disruptive influence, lazy, not getting on and doing anything and bringing the others down'.

Some recognise that the system has now become too punitive. Gareth, in his forties, says:

> Now, apparently, you've got to fill in loads of forms and prove you've been looking for work for about forty hours a week, so it seems much harder to sign on nowadays.

Johnny, an unemployed university graduate in his thirties and renting a room in one of the few Houses of Multiple Occupancy (HMOs) in the street, finds the system Kafkaesque and dysfunctional.

> So you've got, they'll send you on courses to improve your CVs and all that sort of junk, which costs, I don't know how much money, but it's way too much, and they'll employ people to check that you are applying for jobs.

There is passing reference from about a quarter of interviewees to how 'over-generous' welfare benefit regimes were in the past, usually to express support for the current tightened-up regime. But the support is often equivocal. David, a retired medical professional in his seventies, says he does not like the tightened-up regime but he also does not 'like the idea that you could be a total scrounger on the state forever'.

Some participants theorise about unemployment, mentioning terms like 'structural unemployment' or that unemployment can never be zero or that it is a 'tricky' problem (Alan). David says 'ours' has been going down, is a huge issue and 'relates to "the economy"'. Many of them talk of unemployment as a 'social' problem, a 'great social evil' (Michael, in his seventies), leading to 'degeneration' (David, in his seventies). Helen, an accountant in her fifties,[8] elaborates that:

> It does lead to a lot of social problems with people stuck in long-term unemployment; it affects the family and children I mean. Yes it's an economic issue, but I will always feel it's more of a social issue personally.

Jane broadens the effects on immediate family to consider the socio-political phenomenon of the 'left-behind'.

> So unemployment, high levels of unemployment, are socially very destructive... it's not just the lack of money, although that can be extreme, but also the sense of being left behind and not being part of society anymore.

Widespread distrust of employment figures

Many participants from *both* districts mention spontaneously that they do not trust employment statistics and that this distrust is longstanding. Church district participants' comments include the following.

---

[8] Helen does not live in Church district but a similar area.

I don't know what the unemployment figures are, I am told they are going up, but I don't know what people are doing with the statistics they've got. (Rachel, in her fifties)

I think there's a lot more, there's a lot more effective unemployment than is reported. (Peter, retired executive in his seventies)

I think [employment figures] are technically accurate in that they're not sitting around doing nothing, but they haven't got full employment, no, lots of people haven't. (Gareth, in his forties)

I think our unemployment rate has gone down probably over the last ten years but sometimes it's misleading because with any statistics they can change things, can't they? And it's a bit like swapping the figures, for example, the unemployment rate might be a certain percentage and then the government, whichever government happens to be in at the time, decide that anybody who is a job-seeker doesn't get put in the unemployment figures, for example, or anyone who is on short-term sickness or whatever it happens to be. So, maybe the unemployment figures fall, but actually sometimes it's just that a number of people are being categorised in a different way. (Theresa, nurse in her fifties)[9]

Comments from Hill district include more direct references to family members, for example, who have been put on courses. Beverley is particularly angry because of what she sees as courses that have wasted the time and motivation of her grandchildren.

Oh yes, right, that's another thing they say, unemployment. We've brought unemployment down, look at the figures. This is why I don't believe figures. So you look at the figures, yes, that's brilliant, unemployment is come down, not many people are signing on! No, because the reason why is because you've told them they've got to go out and do these things, courses … So when you sign up for this course you come off the unemployment list. So you do all these different courses and that and what happens in the end? You don't get a job! You're unemployed so you go back on the list. So that's where these two lots of figures come in; they've got one lot of figures for unemployment, yet they take the figures off there and say you're doing a course … but really if they were to take them and put them in the proper pile they'd be unemployed. Can you understand what I'm talking about? Does that make sense? (Beverley, in her sixties)

Actually, unemployment, the figures are a load of crap to put it quite crudely, because it tries to fool us that they've accounted for everybody who can't get a job … So there's loads of reasons why we can't get a true figure of unemployment, so basically it's all a big lie whatever figure they come up with … It's all a big con. Which [TV programme] is it, it's on the QI, I think, where you put the Joker up because nobody knows the answer? And I'm putting the Joker up! [Laughs]. (Julie, in her sixties)

[9] Theresa does not live in Church district but a similar area.

Again, they're manipulated depending on how you look at it, depending on what you call employment, who is eligible for employment. So it's very easy to manipulate them, it's no different to an accountant, you can shuffle things around to make the books look good. (Martin, in his fifties)

I don't think they tell the truth about unemployment as well because … they'll say unemployment is this but a lot of those people will be sanctioned, so there will be 1 million people sanctioned, so they'll say 'there's 30 million people are unemployed' or however many, but there should be 1 million more. (Shelley, in her fifties)

Conclusion

There are marked differences between Hill and Church district participants' beliefs about employment.

In Hill district nearly everyone's experience, except for those who have not yet entered the workplace, is of a fairly high degree of job change, including a considerable amount of 're-skilling' and training. Incomes are low and only a couple have ever attempted to buy houses. There is a lot of mention of terms like 'struggle' and 'manage'. Participants are acutely aware of the need to budget. There is *fear* of phenomena like zero hours or unemployment. There is a spectrum of beliefs about those on benefits, ranging from a perception that the regime has become too harsh and is counter-productive, leading to misery and foodbanks, to a belief that some still avoid work, for instance, through having children. However, wherever participants are on that spectrum, they cite personal experience often.

In Church district, there is a pattern of retired professionals believing they are still comfortable and have been lucky to experience secure employment and rising house prices. Some are concerned about their children. For those below retirement age, there is greater diversity in experience; a couple in their thirties and forties have experienced periods of joblessness, a couple some illness. Eighteen-year-olds are convinced they will have less secure employment than their grandparents. Those in the private sector have more in-depth understanding of employment, at least in their sectors, but some Church district participants say they and their families and friends have not experienced poor employment conditions or unemployment issues themselves. They tend to theorise about it and look at the issue from the perspective of the whole of society, calling it in part a social problem.

It is striking that many participants, whether from Hill district or Church district, raise their longstanding distrust of government employment statistics, although on Hill district the distrust is more closely linked to personal experience. I explore trust further in Chapters 6 and 7.

4

'Government debt is not an issue'

Debts are crippling because it's so easy, so, so easy when you're unemployed and you've got no money and somebody says to you 'I'll give you £200 today, you'll pay me back about £400 at £20 a week'. You think 'oh yes God, yes, I can run and go and get £100-worth of shopping in the food cupboard. I can go and get the shoes that the kids need'. And then lo and behold that £20 a week never ends, it never ends … They'll say 'we'll top your loan up. We'll give you another £200 and you pay £800'. And you think, yes! You never hear what you have to pay back because you're so happy to count the money you're getting in your hand. I've been trapped in it for years and years and years… I can't see a way out of it. (Linda, in her fifties, Hill district)

You mustn't be a spendthrift, you need to be quite careful and sure… I don't agree with people being in a lot of debt and I do think, these days, people want things that they can't have. (Rachel, in her fifties, Church district)

These two extracts reveal a divide in what low- and high-income participants believe about personal debt. For Linda, payday loan-style debt to pay for food and bills is to be feared and is also unavoidable. For Rachel, debt could be avoided.

How do participants understand the related issues of personal debt, government debt, tax and spending in Brexit Britain? As I outlined in Chapter 1, for some time in political economic writing there was a dominant thesis that many accepted the pain of austerity cuts in welfare spending because they believed they were necessary to reduce government debt (Blyth 2013; Gamble 2013). Quite often political economists such as Blyth and Gamble have talked about the exist- ence of a 'common sense' understanding that personal debt is morally distasteful and therefore government debt is too. This chapter contributes to debates about austerity by exploring how participants see the connection between personal and government debt and whether there is one common sense, or more than one. As economic and moral reasoning may intersect more in discussion of debt than some of the other topics of the interviews, this chapter also throws some light on where 'economic' as a category begins and ends.

More recently, surveys show that from 2013 acceptance of 'austerity' started to reverse and some argue rising anger about the effects of austerity then motivated lower-income people to vote Leave (Dorling 2016; Berry 2016; Hopkin 2017a), especially as austerity had undermined trust in Osborne and Cameron, the two faces of the Remain campaign, and their 'Project Fear' (Watson 2017).

I set the findings out district by district because the responses of most in Hill district are so different from those in Church district, although I do highlight where patterns between districts are similar and how some individuals' beliefs differ from those of the majority in their district. I start with the findings on debt and government spending, where the differences between districts are most striking, and then go on to taxation.

Hill district

'Fear' of personal debt

The question 'what do you understand about debt?' elicits heartfelt responses in Hill district. I do not stipulate whether I mean personal or government debt because participants' interpretation of the question may itself reveal which is uppermost in their minds. Many in Hill district respond to my neutrally worded question by assuming I mean personal debt, not government or national debt. As Andy in Hill district (in his sixties) immediately says, 'local debt', meaning personal, 'is really bad around here'. I present what Hill district participants understand about personal debt in some detail to provide context for their contrasting understanding of government debt.

I identify the dominant theme that emerges from Hill district as 'fear' of personal debt because fear is an all-encompassing term that incorporates notions like 'trap' and 'horrible' and the pervasive sense that debt may not be far away. Some participants express their fear of personal debt by using words like 'thankfully' (Adam, in his thirties) to describe currently being debt-free, and Lidia, in her forties, is 'so proud now because we haven't got any more loans, we paid it all'.

As I mentioned in Chapter 1, Diane's life (in her thirties) is profoundly affected by housing-related debt. She has only ever earned the minimum wage, working long hours in respite care and as a cleaner as well as caring for her children. She and her partner, a painter and decorator, decided to buy a house when the market was rising. They saved all the deposits and fees, bought the house and then he lost most of his work following the 2008 crash. She says:

> We struggled along, kept trying to pay, finding all the monies, and then we said enough's enough. It was out of our control we were going to lose it so we had to sell it.

They were not profligate in their lifestyle, but were forced to sell the house after only a year at a loss, incurring a debt that they are still paying off eight years later. In this extract from our interview, Diane expresses optimism that in the end they will pay it off but also a weight of revulsion and perhaps shame that 'it' is still there. The quote also shows how the debt controls her and her partner because they feel they have to subject themselves to the debt adviser's direction:

> **Diane**: We got into debt so we're still paying for it now but we'll get there. Yeah.
> **Interviewer**: And did you get any help with that?
> **Diane**: Not really no, just all out of our wages bit by bit what we could afford went into pay plan and paid off, then we got told to come out of that and wait until we had a bit of money behind us so we could keep on top of the bills, and then still pay bills off as and when we can. But there is still debt there.

Out of all the participants, Diane mentions words like 'managing' or 'surviving' most frequently, with several variants of the theme that she just lives from day to day.

Most other participants who have got into debt have got into debt to pay bills. Linda, in her fifties and on benefits and therefore shunned by banks, whose words I include at the head of this chapter, can only borrow from payday lenders. She believes debt is a 'trap'. In Chapter 2 I already mentioned Chris, who got into debt due to benefit non-payment and had no food in the cupboards by the time the bailiffs arrived. I also mentioned Elena, who inherited her parents' debts, along with care of her younger siblings at age nineteen.

Some who believe they have been too materialistic are critical of themselves, such as Julie (in her sixties), who says that when she was depressed she had an attack of 'havingness' consumer spending, and she was only able to clear the debt because she was made redundant. She says in the past people often had to pay up front for things such as electricity on a meter, which reduces temptation to get into debt. She thinks there should be a legal upper limit on payday loan rates.

> To actually protect people from themselves and also to make sure that there's more people in place that are easily accessible when people are starting to get into debt. So this is probably not what you wanted to hear about debt [she knows I probably wanted to hear more about government debt], but that's part of it. I am seriously appalled, they [payday lenders] get 100 per cent, 1000 per cent and people are already seriously, seriously struggling. It's going to push people over the edge into suicide and God knows what.

Martin (in his fifties) blames the broader social context because he thinks material pressures are strong and identifies the 1980s as the point when the 'avoid debt' tradition his working-class parents had grown up with changed.

> I think that [the 1980s expansion in credit] was the biggest change. We were all victims of corporate finance multinational companies especially around that time ... it was rammed that you can own your own house, you can own your own car and everything else, and that was what came from America. It was all on credit,

you know. And before that people didn't have overdrafts, you couldn't get an over-draft if you wanted one, the bank wouldn't do it, but now you can go into debt up to your eyeballs. You end up in a trap. It doesn't help that people are chasing the dream existence. I think they see it on telly all the time. *Relocation* [TV programme] – you look at all the houses so they're always chasing that next goalpost sort of thing, but you become a victim.

Rosa brings in the broader financial system with her belief that:

It's what's sustaining the banks, debt. They like debt.

Martin and some other participants are even more fearful for the younger generation. Rosa has already had to pay her son's debts off twice because he was, in her view irresponsibly, offered credit cards too young. Debt exercises a particular hold over the eighteen-year-old college students interviewed, some of whom are contemplating university. But even here there is a marked distinction between how low-income students contemplate university debt; Clare, who worries about the debt her mother is already in, says of future student loan debt that it is:

Something hanging over your head all the time because money pretty much stresses me out all the time and having that debt, it's just kind of an inevitable thing that we're going to have to deal with.

For a while, Clare's fear of future debt makes her question her desire to go to university. She has already had difficult conversations with her council tenant mother about the financial impact of her leaving because of the bedroom tax. These conversations and doubts are common in her friendship groups. On the other hand, fellow student Phoebe, who sees herself as 'quite privileged', says future debt is not such an 'issue'.

Misha, in her early thirties, is less critical either of herself or society for getting into debt. She jokes about how she cannot curb her interest in 'shiny, new things' and, despite attempts of others to give her debt advice, she just accepts that her debt will probably be a permanent feature in her life.

In summary, most Hill district participants believe life is a struggle and their low incomes and security (see Chapter 3) make them fear debt. Even if they are not living with debt now, they can imagine circumstances where it might be impossible to avoid. They offer often grim narratives of debt as either a consuming addiction or a trap and have sympathy for those, particularly the young, who get lured into it. It is a striking pattern that all those who express 'fear' of personal debt and perceive it as hard to avoid are from Hill district. Contrary to the Gamble (2013) thesis of a moral common sense repugnance towards personal debt, there is not a strong moral component to their comments on personal debt; they just fear it.

'What does government debt even mean?'

Many Hill district participants fear personal debt. What do they believe about government debt? Do they believe the narrative that government debt is a serious issue? Do they support the analogy Conservative politicians in particular often draw between household and government debt – that in the same way a household should cut spending to get out of debt, however painful, so should a government? One example of Osborne (2010) making the analogy is his accusation that the Labour government 'failed to fix the roof when the sun was shining … It's like with a credit card. The longer you leave it, the worse it gets. You pay more interest. You pay interest on the interest. You pay interest on the interest on the interest'. Is this 'household analogy' a form of 'common sense'? Do participants believe that it is morally wrong, as well as being economically damaging, for the *government* to be in debt?

The first theme that emerges is that at least seven Hill district participants are not aware of government debt being serious or problematic, sometimes because they lack any knowledge of it. In response to 'what do you understand about government debt?', Beverley, in her sixties, says:

I'm not quite certain on that, I'm not certain on that.

Gary, a health worker in his forties, says:

I don't understand what the government's debt is to be quite honest. I don't understand enough of it. All you hear is we pay these people this X amount and those people that X amount of money.

Trevor, a retired forklift driver, says:

I don't know a lot about government's debt, you know.

Jean, in her seventies, adds an element of lack of concern.

Aah. I don't know a lot about the debt of the government at all, not really, because I don't take a lot of notice of it.

Elena, in her thirties, is aware but unconcerned.

Interviewer: Have you ever been aware of the country being in debt, the government being in debt?
Elena: Oh apparently, yes apparently, yes everyone says that about borrowing and borrowing too much, yeah.
Interviewer: Does it worry you?
Elena: Not really, not really.

Misha supplies insights into how, when she is not seeking information and using a lot of social media, any information that filters through is likely to be unreliable.

> Government debt? I'd say not really. Again, it's what you hear on social media and you can't always trust … social media and what the news tells you … So I tend to … listen to what I've heard and then sort of like see the outcome myself as opposed to sitting there like 'we're in this amount of debt, we're all going bankrupt'.

Lidia assumes that the UK cannot be in as much debt as her home country, Poland.

> I don't think UK have got that kind of problem, in my country I know … they spend more, especially now with new government, they spend more than they earn.

Linda says in the focus group, in the context of a discussion about government cuts:

> [Mimicking a politician] 'We don't want to leave this country in debt' – why? What does that even mean? Who cares?

In Hill district some are aware of government debt but blame the government for it. There are three 'levels of blame'. First, there are those who believe the government has exaggerated the debt for its own ends. Some, such as Martha, in her forties, interpret former Chancellor of the Exchequer Osborne's motives as attempting to shift blame for the 2008 banking crisis onto the whole population.

> So at one point it was the banks and now it's all us. So it's become more our responsibility and it's kind of the language seems to have affected our psyche in the fact that it's all our responsibility together.

The second level of distrust of government is based on a more generalised distrust of politicians as a class. Linda, in her fifties, distrusts politicians so much she has never voted and would like to start a non-voting campaign.

> I'd love to say to the world 'stop voting'. 'Stop voting' and let's see what happens. Let's see what happens when we stop voting for them arseholes to get rich.

Other participants have always voted. Beverley, in her sixties, describes herself as having inherited a Conservative voting tradition from her father and voted Leave in the referendum, which she is articulate and passionate about. Her civic-mindedness is demonstrated by her role as a kind of citizen auditor for the council. Nevertheless, even though Beverley always votes, she often expresses distrust of politicians (see Chapter 3 on employment statistics). Likewise, Colin (in his sixties) thinks government debt is 'all hidden away'. The government is directly to blame for the debt due to incompetence. Shelley (in her fifties) echoes this, saying:

> Yeah I could understand about how bad the government debt was. I don't know, aren't they to blame, really, the government, for getting us in this situation?

An even stronger third level of 'distrust' is that politicians are lining their own pockets. Jean (in her seventies) says:

> In [Osborne's] pocket yeah! [Laughs]. They run around in these big posh cars, don't they ... they don't have to pay for it. That's right, this is how it goes along.

Elliott (in his seventies) says:

> They're all right. They've got their little contained package and a good pension at the end and handshake but the likes of Joe Public, we never see any of that.

Even if they are aware, or are made aware in the interview, that the government is in debt, none express or recognise the Osborne narrative of the household debt analogy that it is as damaging for a government to get into debt as a household. Many in Hill district believe that personal debt is *more* serious.

In Hill district, there is less support for spending cuts than in Church district. Many feel they have been hit hard by government spending cuts and that these should be reversed. Those who are most concerned about personal debt and on low incomes are least concerned about waste in government spending and want spending to increase. Misha says:

> I don't think you could ever spend too much on schools and hospitals because I think that those are the main things that probably you should be spending [taxes] on, because everybody needs healthcare and everybody needs a fair education.

Rosa echoes participants from both districts when she says the government spends too much on bailing out the banks. Five participants from both districts believe privatisation and contracting out have wasted government money. Rosa notices in her community centre work that the private company supplying services to them is inefficient and unaccountable compared with the old local government employees and that the council has imposed political restrictions on their campaigning work. George, in his seventies, is explicit on the need to 're-nationalise' the NHS.

> I think the NHS needs to be completely re-nationalised and we should also be building more council houses.

There is a theme of comments from Hill district in particular that show strong opposition to austerity and the principle behind austerity – that we could somehow all be 'in it together'. Instead, any version of austerity that includes cutting spending on social services is seen as endangering the social fabric of the country. All those on benefits, including tax credits, report having been hurt by the cuts; Elena (in her thirties) feels 'dread', Gary (in his forties) 'a sinking feeling', some that government is squeezing people who are most vulnerable such as the disabled. Rosa (in her forties) argues that prevention such as Sure Start should not be cut because it is cheaper than remedial measures. A few talk of returns to previous historical times when the division between rich and poor was stark.

In considering spending cuts, Hill district participants are more likely to express frustration that politicians are out of touch. Gary says:

> They have it all backwards, they're not in touch with people, you know.

Misha is one of several to urge politicians to live at least for a while on lower incomes so that they can become better at directing social policy.

> Because I feel like they grow up in such a different world than that which they're trying to impact. 'Okay you lot need to do this, you lot needs to do that.' Have you ever met people like this before? Have you ever experienced what they're doing with their lives? Like, how can you say how they need to live if you have never actually lived in that sort of environment to know whether it affects you or not?

Church district

'Prudent' beliefs about personal debt

Many Church district participants claim to have had 'frugal' childhoods. What do they believe about personal debt? In contrast with Hill district, only one, Mary, admits to ever having had a non-mortgage-related personal debt and that was for £12; even though it was such a small amount, her worry about it is underpinned with moral repugnance. Fawad, in his forties and now in business, and Peter, a retired business executive, say they learned to be prudent.

> So, you know, money was always precious, you had to be prudent. (Fawad)

Theresa,[1] in her fifties, says it 'rubbed off on her' being taught to live within her means.

Rachel, in her quote at the start of this chapter when she says 'people want things that they can't have', brings in the notion of profligacy. Stephanie, a medical professional in her fifties, puts it more strongly in her introduction of a moral element.

> My philosophy would be to decrease the amount that you are in debt because you're a slave to the person to whom you owe money.

In terms of the personal experiences underpinning this perception of debt as profligacy, participants perceive mortgages of an appreciating asset to be distinct from non-mortgage-related debt.

> But anyway, I never had any debt, except a mortgage obviously, for this place, which is now paid off of course. (Joseph)

---

[1] Theresa does not live in Church district but a similar area.

I'm not very good on debt; the only debt I have is my mortgage, never had a loan. (Rachel)

The previous chapter shows they are awed by how much money they have made from their 'debts' in property and conscious their own children may not be so lucky. When they talk about 'undesirable' personal debt, they mean debt due to excessive spending.

'Our country's debt is too high'

Church district participants talk more about government debt in their answers than Hill district participants do. They often assume by my question 'what do you understand about debt?' that I mean government debt and only mention personal debt when I subsequently prompt them.

Unlike Hill district participants, they make strong connections between personal and government debt, supporting the household debt analogy. David, a retired medical professional, says:

> There is a view that you shouldn't spend more than you've got, which logically would certainly apply to me as a private individual. We've never bought anything, except our house, with a debt. If we want a new television we saved the money to get it, if we want a new car everybody said take out a loan. We didn't, we paid cash, we've never owed anything and to my mind, at a simple level I could say it would be nice if the government was in such a situation that they never spent more than they got.

Rachel (in her fifties) says:

> And I've always been brought up, you don't have hire purchase, you pay for what you have and so I think perhaps my gut reaction is the country shouldn't be on too much debt actually. To be honest, yeah, probably I would come down on that.

There is much talk of 'cutting your cloth' and how 'we as a household' would discuss reducing our debt. Fawad (in his forties) says that not 'living beyond your means' is common sense.

> Everyone knows that's good practice, that's the first thing you tell a child, if you want to buy something you save up.

Helen[2] (in her forties) says:

> Yes I do I think it's good not to have any debt. I suppose I tend to think of it like myself; it's important to be a more sustainable economic model and so living within your means is good. So it's a good idea to try and reduce the government debt.

---

[2] Helen does not live in Church district but a similar area.

Again in contrast to Hill district, all except three say the level of government debt is serious, with comments like:

> It's such a big deficit. (Rebecca)

> It's huge [laughs]. And not being paid off. Servicing the debt is, well I couldn't give you any figures, that kind of number in money terms, but it's unimaginable to me. One billion, one thousand million. (Joseph)

> Well it's into trillions, I know that, and increasing because of government spending. (Rachel)

Alan is one of the few with detailed knowledge of the level of government debt.

> Sixty billion a year, which is enormous. If you go back before ten years even, 10 billion deficit per year was seen as very poor but what [Osborne] has done is manage to convince the financial markets that this country is very serious about getting the deficit down, and they've given him the benefit of the doubt, which has kept long-term interest rates down, which has benefited business ... but it could be big problem, could be a real problem if we can't get it down.

Most who acknowledge its size or seriousness support attempts to reduce it.

> Yes, I think so, personally I think it needed to be squeezed and I think [Osborne] did the right thing. (Fawad)

> Yes, yes I think he was right in that ... and it still makes me feel uncomfortable, even though I think we've halved it and not quite sure what we've done but we've made some inroads ... but yes we did need to get deficit down. (Harry)

I ask participants what they understand about government spending to context-ualise their beliefs about austerity. There are many comments that reflect a desire to reduce expectations of what the government can achieve. This is sometimes linked with the belief that excessive personal spending and debt reflects unreal-istic expectations, as in Rachel's comment:

> I think overall we have to reduce our expectations of what is possible in order to reduce our [government] debt, we can't have it both ways.

This is echoed by Stephanie (in her fifties) on government spending, that:

> Our expectations are greater than they ever have been ... I think our country's debt is too high.

In contrast to Hill district there is far more spontaneous mention of waste in response to my question 'what do you know and understand about government spending?' Alan (in his forties) shows unease when he says:

> I'm not opposed to government spending rising, if I was sure it was being spent wisely, but I don't think it is.

James (in his seventies) thinks:

> There are things that the government needs to do, but it seems to be wasteful.

Fawad says:

> There's a lot of inefficiencies like I said in the scheme of things and personally I think the NHS could be better run.

Rebecca echoes this theme on waste, as on a recent hospital visit she thought:

> Couldn't they do this a bit more efficiently?

However, despite the beliefs of some that government spending is too high and wasteful, leading to support for cuts in spending, there is also unease about cuts. Some mention that Osborne promised everyone would be 'in it together' in his version of austerity but in reality it affects the poor more than the rich. Harry comments 'the idea that we were in it altogether was important', but:

> I don't feel that was carried through, because the difference in wages is showing that it's ... become rather impossible for some people at the bottom of the pile. I'm not sure that's really been understood ... The way in which austerity hits the poor is very regrettable and ... we're going to get a lot of very alienated people with impossible situations.

Teacher Rebecca, in her fifties, echoes concerns about long-term costs of austerity.

> I thought it was quite a good thing, but then to get the deficit down you have to stop spending so much on other things and when they're things like Sure Start or whatever, then you kind of think well those kind of things might seem like a good economy, but actually the repercussions are ... those children, those families, are not supported perhaps further down the line. There will be family breakdown and then the state will have to pay.

Rachel (in her fifties) and some other older Church district participants identify the problem with austerity's implementation as a lack of social cohesion more generally. The British people no longer unite to sacrifice for the common good in part because class divisions have become more acute.

> Because I don't think we feel part of the club, because we are a class society we don't have this feeling of we are in this together.

Nevertheless, however uneasy, Rachel concludes:

> I do think, I do think we should have had austerity.

Stephanie (in her fifties), after expressing similar unease, also ends with:

> But I still believe the government should be balancing its books and not borrowing.

'People know how to fiddle the taxes'

Beliefs about tax are relevant to debt and government spending because raising them is an alternative to spending cuts as a debt reduction measure. Answers to questions on tax are less patterned according to district than on spending or debt. Not all participants pay income-related taxes, even though they do all pay direct taxes such as VAT. However, whilst people who pay income tax complain more about 'rip-off' taxes (Rosa) than those who do not, there is a dominant pattern of criticism of tax avoidance.

In answer to the question 'what do you know and understand about tax?' over twenty participants from both districts voluntarily mention unprompted tax evasion or avoidance by companies and individuals. It is dominant in the news, particularly in the early part of the interview period. Therefore there is a theme running through many interviews that some government debt could be reduced by clamping down on tax avoidance.

From Hill district, Chris, in his sixties, now on disability benefit and previously a taxi driver, says:

> But people know how to fiddle the taxes, you know, even with self-employed taxi drivers … and I think to myself I don't know how they do it.

Other comments include:

> The people at the top, because I used to work for them, don't pay any or they try to get away with paying zero. They do as little as possible for the country most of them, it's all in their pocket … I do know people that don't pay any and they're absolutely minted. It's disgusting. (Colin, in his sixties)

> Rich families … are not paying the tax and this is not a good policy for the poor people. (Mona, in her thirties)

> And then you got the whole debacle of tax avoidance. (Martha, in her forties)

Church district participants are also outraged.

> I mean they're supposedly getting away with paying little or no tax on a certain part of their income. (Mary, in her seventies)

> And I know it's very difficult to say what is a reasonable arrangement of one's affairs in the light of the whole taxation situation of the country and what is aggressive tax avoidance, but I do think that there are moral issues. (Michael, in his seventies)

Where I feel very upset about taxation is the fact that in recent years corporations have been able to drive a coach and horses through the laws and avoid paying taxes so they benefit from society, they benefit from all the things that are provided by society but they don't pay towards it and that seems to me fundamentally unfair. (Peter, in his seventies)

Nearly as many of the total sixty participants, seventeen, believe that the tax burden has shifted too far from the rich and that they should be liable to pay more. This comment by Hill district's Julie, reflects that view:

I think years and years ago the really rich people were well and truly hammered, in the old money every nineteen [shillings] and six I think went on tax and the six pennies they kept. Well, never should that have ever happened, but at the same time it's gone too far the other way now and there's too many loopholes and the very rich seem to know how to use them. Quite frankly the country needs all of the money! The very rich people, there's only so many houses they need whether they like it or not. They would say they've been gifted to earn so much money, why don't they just put up what they should be paying and that's that! (Julie, in her sixties)

Some, more in Hill district than Church district, argue that the level of tax is too low.

The rich people are taxed for a certain percentage. I know they say they've got to protect them around London because otherwise they'll move abroad and everything else. How true is that? We don't know. (Martin, in his fifties)

Rachel is among those in Church district who worry that tax is still too high for those on low incomes, which will disincentivise work.

I do think that the base rate [threshold] should be much higher ... for people who are working and on low incomes, because I know salaries haven't gone up for a long time and people can't make ends meet.

Whilst not all participants advocate increasing taxes on the rich, only four out of the sixty participants oppose doing so.

'Borrow to invest' support for Keynesianism

There is a group composed of participants from both districts who *explicitly* reject Osborne's household analogy – a group of ten who reject it because they support the Keynesian alternative. The Keynesian approach is that government debt, particularly if it is to finance infrastructure investment, should not always be perceived as a problem and these participants can be described as explicitly Keynesian in a combined rejection of the household debt analogy and using spending cuts to reduce debt. They argue from a basis of economic knowledge of the Keynesian alternative and therefore undermine the thesis (Blyth 2013; Hay

2010:467) that people find it harder to understand than 'simple' pro-austerity arguments. Paul[3] (in his fifties) says:

> I think as individuals we are always reluctant to be in debt, but for the country, you know, it's a way of building the economy.

Jane is another example.

> I know that there is an economic theory which says that if you are in low growth you should spend your way out of the difficult situation by going into debt to finance, for example, infrastructure projects in order to create employment, so that people will earn money and spend that, and that will somehow boost the economy. I suppose on a personal level running your own budget going into debt and having a deficit is always worrying, but I think that on a national level it is a completely different matter.

All ten, from both districts, see themselves as left of centre and show throughout their interviews that they are politically engaged.

Only a couple of participants support the Hay/Blyth thesis that Keynesianism is hard to understand; they want to believe in the Keynesian argument, which they are vaguely aware of, but they express a lack of confidence in their understanding of the detail of it. This view is expressed clearly by David, who mentions:

> These economic mechanisms, which I really don't understand, you know the idea that if you spend more and borrow more you can borrow out of debt.

He knows some economists dispute the 'austerity' approach but 'that's when I begin to not understand'. He also expresses anxiety about this division between economists in itself, a theme echoed by many others throughout the interviews, which I cover in Chapter 6.

Conclusion

Many participants over forty, whether from low- or high-income backgrounds, inherited a tradition to be prudent and avoid debt. However, adult life has thrown up economic dilemmas that, particularly in the case of Hill district participants, have forced a readjustment. Most Hill district participants have some experience of personal debt in their families. In some cases it is through consumerism, but in other cases because they inherit it, were affected by 2008 or do not have enough wages or benefits to pay essential bills. Their debt often takes the form of payday loans. They fear personal debt as something they may be forced into.

How far does this chapter support the claim (Blyth 2013; Gamble 2013) that there was a dominant pro-austerity 'common sense' based on morality and

---

[3] Paul does not live in Church district but a similar area.

economic understanding? This chapter supports their argument *for the higher-income groups* (Stanley 2014). However, these interviews show that there are differences in the content of the moral and economic everyday understanding between the two districts. Hill district everyday economic understanding of personal debt is different – it is far less 'avoidable' and also hard to reduce. Hill district participants' moral understanding of personal debt is also different. They do not use much moral terminology in their discussion of debt. They see personal debt as more of a problem than government debt. They are also less keen to cut government spending and they distrust austerity compared with those in Church district.

In short, these interviews show that many Hill district participants do not have the 'common sense' that Blyth and Gamble describe that supports the need for spending cuts to reduce 'morally repugnant' government debt. These findings show the importance of conducting in-depth interviews with people from lower-income backgrounds, whose voices are often not heard as strongly by political scientists.

In contrast, Church district participants have a 'common sense' that is similar to that described by Blyth and Gamble. Most in Church district do see debt as profligacy, and, for the overwhelming majority, the only debt they have ever accumulated is a mortgage on what has turned out to be a safe and ever-appreciating asset. The debt that other people have that worries them is debt due to spending that they do see as profligate – expectations need to be reined back in, both of standards of living and of what governments can provide. Church district participants are far more likely to recognise and express support for Osborne's use of the household debt analogy than those in Hill district. They are also more likely to believe that some spending cuts, particularly as there is some waste in the system, are necessary. However, many are uneasy about the scale of the cuts and the perception that the rich have not shared the pain with the poor. This unease may have grown over time as the cuts progressed, outweighing their original unease about the debt.

In Chapter 1 I outlined the neoclassical economists' tendency to believe all non-economists, but particularly those with lower incomes and with fewer years in education, lacked understanding. There were echoes of this in the Gamble (2013), Hay (2010) and Blyth (2013) thesis that economic ideas, such as the household debt analogy, appeal more to people if they are 'simple'. There is only limited support, from a couple of participants, for the argument that participants found the Keynesian argument about austerity less simple than Osborne's approach. Instead, participants fall into three broad groups. The first have not considered the issues of government debt, the second have considered them and agree with Osborne so strongly that the complexity of the Keynesian alternative might not make a difference and the third have made the effort to understand the Keynesian alternative without too much difficulty.

These findings on the debt, government spending and taxation sections of the interviews suggest that cultural and economic beliefs are entwined but that there are striking differences between Hill and Church district participants in *how* they are entwined. Arguably, in this case Church district participants, with their stronger moral repugnance of debt, bring morals into their economic reasoning more than Hill district participants do.

5

Trade and migration: 'other people'

Field diary entry two days after the 2016 referendum

On a warm day in late June it takes me forty minutes to walk the back way to the park, along small Victorian terraces, mostly rented out. The park is a mix of children's playground, tennis courts and a walkway with some lawn, lots of well-kept tropical plants. The café is in the park. It is billed as a community café and has only a small inside area with a large outside wooden patio. While I drink coffee on the patio two men approach, probably father and son, who look as if they have been drinking. They are waiting for something, turns out to be a taxi. The father points, to indicate they should sit down on two of the café chairs and the son says 'we can't just sit there'. But his dad says 'yes we can, England for the English!' He then follows this with an argument loud enough for me to hear: that the café has been set up with lottery money but that it is expensive, too expensive for people like them. Then a taxi pulls up and they get in.

After meeting the café's community worker, I walk from the park in a different direction, now between high-rise, grey pebble-dash council flats and then along the local high street. There are flags hanging out of windows, both St George and Polish. There are a couple of young men who seem menacing. The shops are mainly charity or discount supermarket. There is not much soul. After fifteen minutes I pass three prosperous looking and well organised Polish shops, butcher and grocer – and a post office with beautiful photos of the Polish countryside emblazoned on its shopfront.

This extract from my field diary two days after the referendum, just as I was starting fieldwork, captures how much of a shock the referendum result was. People who did not usually talk about politics were engaged, excited or scared. The referendum followed years of high levels of migration from Eastern Europe into the city. There were Polish and Russian neighbourhoods and Polish shops. There were some native-born who resented it. However, there were others who welcomed it. Employer Alan stressed what he perceived as the greater desirability of migrants as employees. He was pleased that migration from Eastern Europe had brought in 'lively, educated people'.

The three themes of this chapter are: first, understanding of trade, second, understanding of the economic effects of migration and third, how people evaluate their own political behaviour as economic.

Trade

When I ask interviewees 'what do you know and understand about trade?' they say less about trade than on any of the other seven components of 'the economy' I ask them about. Using NVivo I find the length of their answers is *half* that of their answers on employment or migration, for example. In addition, with a few exceptions, they do not draw on personal experience in their answers.

Hill district

'I'M NOT SURE ABOUT TRADING'

Several Hill district participants say they do not understand much about trade. Jean's only response to my question is to talk about whether there are foreign tomatoes in the shops. Misha (a non-voter but Remain supporter in her thirties), says 'I don't really know much about it'. Adam (a Remain voter in his thirties), says he knows nothing about trade even though in the rest of his interview he talks about how Brexit will damage the motor manufacturing sector's prospects; he does not connect the two concepts. Shelley (a non-voter in her fifties), says:

> I don't know really a lot about Europe and trading. I know we trade a lot to them so I don't know if we can still do that [post-Brexit]. I'm not sure about trading to be honest.

Rosa (a Remain voter in her forties) says she knows nothing, despite having a lot to say on nearly every other economic concept.

Most of the eighteen-years-olds also respond saying they do not understand much about trade. Lisa, aged eighteen, excuses her lack of knowledge about trade by saying:

> I think it's just because it doesn't have much of an impact on my life. It probably does, but, in my eyes, not much impact on me.

Eighteen-year-old Clare,[1] who gives full answers on other issues, flounders when she says the only mention she heard of trade was by her uncle, who owned a shop. He told her we would still be able to trade post-Brexit. She comments:

> I thought that might have been a bit not necessarily correct, because if we left the EU then how willing would members of the EU be to trade with us?

---

[1] Clare does not live in Hill district but a similar area.

I divide the rest of the Hill district participants' comments on trade according to whether they are broadly in favour of maintaining the current EU-based trade regime or not.

NON-EU STATES 'DON'T ACTUALLY MAKE WHAT WE WANT'

From Hill district, the majority of the interviewees who express support for staying in the EU trading regime, all Remainers, are qualified or pragmatic rather than principled. Colin (in his sixties) has a narrow conception of the benefits of free trade within the EU when he stresses the benefits of it '*to the UK*'. He also has some criticisms of the EU trade regime, saying it worked when it was a union of twelve nations but now poorer EU nations drag it down. Martin (in his fifties) is also pragmatic; he quotes the figures that show we do a far greater proportion of trade with the EU than the USA and comments that Leave supporters 'said we can trade with all these other people but, no you can't, because they don't actually make what we want'. He and several others argue that there is no point in looking to the Commonwealth nations for deals because they are either too small or have moved on.

Lidia (in her forties), a long-term resident originally from Poland, echoes how positive common EU standards are; she is conscious that the UK 'shares norms' with the rest of the EU on subjects like workers' rights that other non-EU trading partners might not respect. It is interesting that she is the only participant to refer explicitly to Europeans sharing norms.

NON-EU STATES 'ARE LINING UP TO DO TRADE WITH US'

Apart from Julie, who acknowledges it will be an 'uphill struggle', most Leave supporters are positive about trade prospects post-Brexit, including believing American and Commonwealth deals will be lucrative. The most positive about the effects of Brexit on trade include George (in his seventies) who believes that because the UK is a net importer from the EU, the EU will not impose tariffs for fear of retaliation:

> When it comes to trade, I don't think there's going to be any problems; we've already got countries lining up to do trade with us.

Steven (in his eighties) echoes George's optimism, believing the UK will be 'better off' out of the EU due to its skills and talent. Elliott (in his seventies) says trade was killed off by the Thatcher government closure of the manufacturing and heavy industry, which has led to us being flooded by cheap Chinese imports and becoming a 'satellite' of Europe. Whilst not explicit, he blames the EU for the flooding component of that argument. Beverley (in her sixties) says those who argue other countries will not make trade deals with the UK are talking 'rubbish

... you don't know what's going to happen'. Gary (in his forties) describes the single market as 'mates' rates discount' and says we will not get such a good discount with the EU after we leave, but:

> We can make new deals with other people. There are a lot of countries in the world who would be happy to deal with us.

Beverley, George and Elliott, when they meet in a focus group several months later, are still optimistic about trade deals post-Brexit.

The comments by Leave voters who do not believe UK trade will be significantly damaged by Brexit because it will trade with the Commonwealth nations are worth quoting in full.

- Beverley (in her sixties): 'Remainers are wrong to say "oh well, when you come out you won't be able to go to, like, New Zealand, and different places like that".'
- Elena (in her thirties): America and New Zealand 'want to trade with us'.
- George (in his seventies): 'We used to have, we used to be part of the biggest trading bloc in the world, which was the Commonwealth, and now we're the fifth- or sixth-biggest. I don't know, but if you go back to the Commonwealth we'll be the biggest again'.
- Trevor (in his seventies): 'Before we went into [the EU] we used to trade a lot with the Commonwealth, New Zealand, Australia, South Africa'.

Nearly all those mentioning the Commonwealth are over fifty. Points to note about these comments are that:

- participants who want trade with the Commonwealth do not tend to mention wanting trade with China, Indonesia or other non-Commonwealth countries;
- there is not much explicit reference back to any history before World War II in the interviews; these interviewees, nearly all over 60, are referring to the Commonwealth as they personally remember it.

Church district

As in Hill district, Church district participants also lack understanding of trade, whether Leavers or Remainers. Only a couple mention issues like services or the longstanding trade deficit. Again the lack of in-depth understanding of the place of trade in 'the economy', even among supporters of the current trade regime, is striking.

FREE TRADERS

Out of the fifteen interviewees who broadly want to keep the current trading situation, only a few express belief in the principle of both trade and free trade as positive. Church district's Alan (in his forties) is an economic liberal strongly committed to the principle of free trade. He is one of the few who offers in-depth factual knowledge. He sees the EU customs union as 'a very positive element'; even though he criticises the EU's high external tariff on agricultural imports from less economically developed countries, he thinks the EU has been moving in the right direction to rectify that. He also believes the European customs union has the potential to be transferred to a global stage leading to the desirable prospect of global free trade. He wanted a 'tariff-free world where everyone's incomes were more the same and hopefully ... rising to a level as they are in Western countries at the moment'.

Fawad, also in his forties and directly involved in the manufactured exports business, shows a similar degree of commitment to international collaboration and the need to export and is in despair about what he sees as a lack of government awareness about how tough trade negotiations are likely to be. David (in his seventies) may not have been directly involved in trade but has a liberal commitment to the principle of trade as 'a good thing'. Paul (in his fifties), a trade union employee, conceives of trade as positive but differs from the liberals in perceiving the single market and customs union as positive because of regulation of food and employment standards at the EU level.

A few others also express reservations about trade deals with authoritarian regimes. At least three have in-depth awareness of TTIP[2] negotiations between the USA and the EU. They believe aspects of it have damaging implications for democracy that highlight the dangers of doing trade deals post-Brexit.

BREXIT OPPORTUNITY

Those against the EU trade regime, Leave voters, tend to emphasise how speculative economists' warnings are about leaving the EU. James (in his seventies) says the EU's external tariffs on imports are low and says the devaluation of the pound may make our exports cheap enough to offset it. Harry (in his fifties) says 'we *could* get much better deals [my italics]' outside the EU and, like the Hill district Leavers, mentions the Commonwealth.

> So trade I think there's immense potential, immense opportunity and that, provided we don't talk ourselves out of confidence, that could be a very great opening out as a result of us not being controlled by European government. (Harry, in his fifties)

Their comments are usually couched within the overall thesis that, as Harry comments, we must not 'talk ourselves out of confidence'. The context for the

---

[2] The Transatlantic Trade and Investment Partnership (TTIP) negotiations between the USA and the EU were prominent in the news and controversial because they were perceived as increasing corporate power to reduce the scope of government policy.

comments is that even if there is a small amount of damage to trade, it will be worth it. In other words, the impression is less of a hankering back than a desire to rationalise putting sovereignty above economics, again reflected in Harry's comments about the 'opening out' as a result of not being 'controlled by European government'.

Migration

Hill district

In Hill district there is a variety of beliefs about migration. Fourteen of the thirty Hill district participants, mainly older, believe migration has negative economic effects and express this consistently. They include four black and ethnic minority participants and some Remain voters. Eight Hill district participants are ambivalent or non-committal or believe that the economic damage from migration is slight. Eight Hill district participants, mainly the higher-income and younger ones, believe that migration benefits 'the economy', which is a lower proportion than in Church district.

'THEY'RE TAKING OUR KIDS' JOBS'

Nearly all Hill district participants expressing economic arguments against migration mention migrants competing for jobs and resources. Mona and her partner Azad, who emigrated to the UK ten years ago and are two of the Hill district participants most aware of the value of trade and believe the EU customs union benefits 'the economy', are nevertheless so concerned about the negative economic effects of migration on competition for jobs and housing that they voted Leave in the referendum.

> If [migration] carries on like this, lots of people won't be able to have a better life. Based on that, I said no [voted Leave] so it [migration] wouldn't be carried on forever. It's not going to be practically possible to accommodate everyone here. (Azad, in his thirties)

Many spontaneously bring up migration in their responses to my 'what do you understand about employment?' question, and see employment and migration as linked. Chris (in his sixties) says 'my son … he can't find work because of all these foreigners that's coming in and taking jobs'. George (in his seventies) says 'when we've got less people living here we'll have a bigger percentage of them in work'. Howard[3] (eighteen years old) says 'if there's more people there's going to be less jobs' and Jean (in her seventies) says 'they're just taking our kids' jobs'.

---

[3] Howard does not live in Hill district but a similar area.

Some participants argue that migrants 'take jobs' because they are prepared to work for lower pay, not because they are better qualified or have a better work ethic. Linda disagrees with claims that migrants are better workers or 'do jobs that other people don't want to do'. She says there are many British-born who, with encouragement, could do those jobs, but migrants are employed because they are prepared to live in poor conditions for a few years in order to send wages home that are far in excess of anything they would earn there. She says:

> It's just that I think rich people take advantage of the poor people in ways of cheap labour you know … We don't get the opportunity to have the jobs because we have to work for a proper wage to live and they don't want anybody to do that, they want cheap labour.

Many interviewees believe there is a link between migration, low wages and the growth of zero hours' contracts (see Chapter 3). Martin (in his fifties) thinks migration has 'partially' reduced low-skilled wages and businesses are 'clever' – 'so if you've got a guy willing to work for £6 why are you going to pay somebody £8?' Andy (in his sixties) argues that:

> The local people [long-term or native-born residents] don't want minimum wages, they want a liveable wage, whereas the Eastern Europeans, to them it's probably a lot more money they're getting abroad. So they're obviously thinking, 'this is not bad, we can live with this, still send money back'. And I can sympathise with them, but, by the same token, we gotta look after our own.

A related theme is that migrants from the rest of the EU may be benefiting from welfare services and job opportunities without intending to make a permanent commitment to the country as a whole. Ruby says of her co-workers from other EU states that they often talk of the land they own and houses they are building back home.

> I mean they work hard here to send money back home … I think the majority of the guys I work with at work, they will eventually go back.

In this exchange in a Hill district focus group, one of the strands in the argument is that migration is 'making' UK-born workers lazy.

Beverley: … [Migration] is making our people lazy. Our people think, 'oh well, we'll get the Polish, get the whatever… They will work [hard]'. Because my nephew was the manager of a hotel … he knew that the people coming in would work harder and they would get the job done properly …
Elliott: this is why you employ them, to do a good job …

Beverley: the lazy [UK-born workers] should be made to work for their money and to pay taxes.

Elena, in her thirties, volunteers a distinction that skilled migration is more welcome than unskilled. But it is striking that most Hill district participants who perceive migration as increasing competition for jobs talk only in terms of low-skilled work.

'DRAINING RESOURCES'

Many Hill district participants who believe migration overall is economically damaging, and even some who think overall it is beneficial, are concerned about pressures on resources of social housing, school places, health care and benefits.

It is hard to disentangle anecdotal exaggeration from more direct experience. Beverley (in her sixties) says 'people *were* coming over here and getting houses' [my emphasis] but she knows, because she is part of a council citizens audit group, that 'we've now made it' so they have to be here three years before they get social housing. Nevertheless, she still opposes migration because of her personal experience of continuing lack of resources, including children and grandchildren on social housing waiting lists. Her final comment on the issue is 'we can't house our own people, how can we house thousands?' This suggests even the three-year rule is not enough to reassure her that migrants are not taking scarce resources she would prefer to go to native-born.

Chris, in his sixties, also has daughters on the waiting lists and it makes his 'blood boil … when you see the amount of foreign people in council places'. He observes how many buildings locally are also being turned into student accommodation, a preoccupation shared by Linda. Chris contrasts the current housing shortage with:

> When I was young there was loads of council houses being built and all that and they're not building council property anymore … and a lot of these council houses now have been sold off to these coloured people and they rent them out to students and all that.

A few mention school places and overcrowded GPs' surgeries, but, apart from housing, the other competition most people mention is for resources in the shape of benefits. Many are aware of media coverage claiming that migrants send a high proportion of child benefit received in the UK back home. There is little support for migrants being able to claim benefits. Misha (in her thirties) describes herself as even-handed, the child of a Jamaican father who can see that tougher migration controls might have prevented him coming here. However, she says:

I can understand how financially it could drain the system willy nilly, letting people come in and letting people just claim from us and use the resources that we have, like, sending it off back to home.

In her other comments, she could hardly be interpreted as being racist or xeno-phobic. Similarly, Gary (in his forties) has many non-EU migrant friends where he works and does not make any other comments that indicate he opposes migra-tion on socio-cultural grounds, but he says in principle:

Same as if I went to another country I'd expect to work hard and not [for the gov-ernment] to say 'there you go, there's some dole money'.

Shelley (in her fifties) echoes the opposition to paying migrants benefits when she says in answer to whether migration has damaged 'the economy' economically:

Yeah, 100 per cent yes. I don't know all the ins and outs and I don't know if obvi-ously the people who come in to work they pay taxes... but there's so many that don't, there's so many that come ... and claim benefits for the kids that are in their country as well. That's got to do some damage economically really.

'AN ISLAND NATION'

In a Hill district focus group George is anxious that opposition to migration should not be perceived as racist because 'it's actually pure mathematics'. As Elliott agrees, 'the thing is, we are an island nation'. There is a distinct group who dwell on the physical overcrowding of the island. It is striking that they are mainly over sixty. They often use the phrase that migration is 'swamping' the island. I interpret this response, in part, as an economic understanding because they perceive migration as leading to overpopulation and strain on infrastruc-ture. Some would counter that in this virtual and technological globalised age a rich economy would still be able to provide, but these participants disagree. Glenn (in his sixties) says 'you can't get a pint into a half pint... there's not enough land for a dear old grandma to take a dog for a walk or the children to kick a ball around'. Elliott says:

They are trying to push people in here, we are only an island, there is only so much of an area where we can produce food and everything else, because the more we are buying in the more it's costing us the money that could be saved ... There's got to be a cut-off point at some stage. (Elliott, in his seventies)

George (in his seventies) says:

Unfortunately, it's just sheer numbers now that are defeating the infrastructure ... it's nothing to do with nationality, it's to do with numbers of people. We're an island, we've got to remember that, we can't cope.

Julie (in her sixties) reiterates the strain on the infrastructure. Maxine is the only younger person who echoes this theme when she talks about there not being enough 'space'. However, her comment is brief and not as heartfelt as those of older people.

In the interviews, I phrase the question 'what do you understand about the *economic* effects of migration?' specifically to focus on any economic beliefs interviewees may have about the issue. What pictures do participants have in their minds when they hear the word 'migration'? Possibly because the referendum debate was about EU migration and the city has had a big increase in EU migration, most relate my question to migration from the EU rather than, for instance, war-torn Syria. Nevertheless, some Hill district participants mention these *cultural* anti-migration beliefs, sometimes about non-EU migrants, mixed in with their economic ones.

> The Muslims, they come over, they've been living here for years and then they're trying to tell us how to live in our country because it doesn't suit their religion. That is all wrong as well. Obviously we welcome them and have done for years, but they seem to tell us that we are doing it all wrong and if we don't change then they're going to kick us out. I just don't see the point. (Elliott, in his seventies)

> When I was younger I think we had two families living in our street [in London]. They were coloureds and they were great, lovely people, but when I moved out… who you see over there now, you've got every creed. People from Saudi Arabia, they've got cafes along the road, on the pavement, X road, took it over! All cafes, all foreigners you know. They walk past you as if you shouldn't be there, you know, and that is wrong. That is wrong. I wouldn't like to see any trouble start, but I can see it. (Steven, in his eighties)

> I don't mind letting some in, not loads of them, as long as they abide by our rules. What annoys me, and I know my wife too, is they come in here but they want to carry on as if they're still living in their own country … and some of them don't speak English, so you think they should learn English. (Trevor, in his seventies)

> And because my dad was always against them because he fought in the war and all that, he said that's what we fought for, you know. (Chris, in his sixties)

> If they stay here, are they going to be taught different languages? I don't mean like we do now, but [my granddaughter] will come home talking something I won't understand. (Beverley, in her sixties)

All these participants are over sixty. Younger Hill district participants in favour of migration mention a recurring theme of older people, as Rosa says, being manipulated or 'tricked by their own fears' about the effects of migration into voting to Leave. These younger participants emphasise that older participants are afraid of migration, believing media stories of the effect on the benefit bill, for example. Misha (in her thirties) and Shelley (in her fifties), despite themselves saying in places that migration is a strain on the benefits bill, identify older people as being in this 'anti-migration' category.

> **Shelley**: Yes, definitely. I totally agree with that, that's why I'm on about, that's why a lot of people … voted to get out, like the *older generation* [my italics].
>
> **Misha**: It's fear! … [they think migrants] get about twenty grand when they come into this country. What about, okay, the government's going to hand over to someone as they come into the country twenty grand: 'here's twenty grand babe, a BMW and a nice four-bedroomed house'! [Laughs] It's not going to happen, it's just unrealistic but *some people* believe that [my italics].

Some in Hill district believe the economic effects of migration are positive. Hill district participants Lidia and Colin mention that we need more migrants for health and social care. Rosa, in her forties, states vehemently that she 'didn't get' the argument that migration damages 'the economy'. She adds 'there were a lot of economists who have done the figure crunching and say actually, no, they're not draining the society'.

Of the eighteen-year-old low-income participants, nearly all believe migration is both economically and socio-culturally beneficial. Callum[4] is most clear that the economic arguments against migration are spurious.

> When I took GCSE Geography there was a lot of talk about migration so I am aware that the media makes it a lot more worse than it is. It's 'they're stealing our jobs', that kind of thing. It's not like that.

Lucas[5] (eighteen years old) says migrants are 'not taking away from anything, they're giving back as well'. He and Clare both have an additional self-interest in opposing Brexit. Lucas wanted to study in Germany, which is now in jeopardy; he believes older Leave voters are 'wasting an opportunity that's not given to most countries … just seizing up the chances for the younger generation'. Clare[6] (eighteen years old) says her main reason for supporting Remain is educational; she wanted to benefit from the Erasmus scheme.

A common belief from the low-income 18-year-olds is that they did not pay attention to any economic arguments about migration because they just do not see migration as 'an issue'. Callum adds:

[4] Callum does not live in Hill district but a similar area.
[5] Lucas does not live in Hill district but a similar area.
[6] Clare does not live in Hill district but a similar area.

I'm friends with a few people who have moved here and we don't really talk about it because we don't see a problem in it.

Lisa[7] says:

Where with the EU referendum they tried to make it 'oh we'll stop immigration' I didn't really see an issue with that. I don't really think there is an issue with migration and immigration.

She adds that she has not considered the economic arguments about migration because:

Immigration stuff doesn't scare me or anything. I think it is an older generation thing … it doesn't bother me; I think it's a good idea.

Church district

'LOSING OUR BRITISHNESS'

Like Hill district participants, those in Church district also reveal a variety of beliefs. Several make comments about the negative socio-cultural effects of migration.

Alice, in her eighties, says:

I don't mind migrants if they come to England and take on our ideas and our way of life but buying and selling wives and all that jazz is not British and I think we are losing our Britishness, I really do.

Stephanie, in her fifties and a health professional, argues that there is an additional burden on the health service due to differing cultural expectations. Harry, also in his fifties, is torn because he values Britain's Christian heritage, including a tradition of welcoming refugees, but says:

It has potential, particularly jihadist migration, of being incredibly disruptive and it will be interesting to see what effect having open borders has from that point of view. But this is an incredibly difficult subject.

However, some Church district participants who perceive migration as culturally damaging do so because they believe *other people* do not want it and, therefore, too much migration will impose a strain on society as a whole. This is evident in this focus group exchange.

Peter: Migration does worry me and I think unconstrained migration will cause social unrest and that's my main worry. It's not affecting me personally because I'm not in competition for a job with people who are migrating

---

[7] Lisa does not live in Hill district but a similar area.

from other countries. I am quite happy to go and consider that I might go live and work or have a holiday in another country. So I think in general I'm not against migration ... but I can see that uncontrolled and unrestrained migration could lead to very great social stresses and I'm very worried about that – although it doesn't threaten me personally at the moment, but it could do.

Interviewer: So in some ways, whatever the economic arguments about migration, for you there is quite a big social element?

Peter: I think it's mainly social actually.

James: There are economic arguments about how much can the infrastructure stand and so on, but it's a political-sociological issue mainly.

In contrast, some Church district participants are positive about the socio-cultural effects of migration. Alan (in his forties) says 'the idea of a world where people can move from country to country as they choose is very positive ... we are one world, we are one people'. He would only baulk at the numbers if they were in the tens of millions. David (in his seventies) is 'fairly pro-migration', as is Fawad (in his forties). Jane (in her seventies) says it 'improves cultural diversity'; Joseph (in his seventies) says he is 'tolerant' because his parents came from 'penniless Ireland'; Johnny (in his thirties) has 'never seen a gain from divisiveness'.

OVERLOADING THE INFRASTRUCTURE AND 'GEOGRAPHICALLY SMALL'

Some, including Remainers, in Church district do believe migration damages 'the economy'. As James mentions, there are some concerns about the impact of high migration on the infrastructure; while 'the economy' may need young workers, they will grow old or bring families. When I ask Stephanie (in her fifties) what she understands about unemployment, she says 'that all comes into the migration discussions'. Richard (in his eighties) mentions the smallness of the country and fears of an 'open-door' policy: 'small country, geographically small, we've got a pretty high population already'.

Church district participants do not talk from personal experience as much as Hill district ones about the effects of migration on resources. Some interviewees (Peter, Rachel) from Church district are conscious that the area is wealthy enough that numbers of recent migrants moving in are low and services have not been overloaded, therefore that they do not have personal experience of recent low-skilled migration, except as employers. Michael describes Church district as a 'white bubble ... with some Asians ... a conservation area'. Those who do move in to Church district, for example in university-related jobs, are welcomed in part because their numbers are few.

'LIVELY, EDUCATED PEOPLE': MIGRATION BENEFITS 'THE ECONOMY'

A larger proportion in Church district than in Hill district believes migration benefits 'the economy'.

Those who elaborate on the economic benefits of migration tend to express beliefs that can be categorised either as economic self-interest in the free movement within the EU or the benefit to 'the economy' as a whole.

On the self-interest side, several Church district residents have worked abroad, in Asia, America and East Africa, for instance, and have children who work abroad including in Europe. Many of the younger interviewees echo Hill district participants' talk of lessons in geography or history which taught them that migration was part of a two-way relationship. They want to be able to benefit from free movement themselves.

> I wouldn't necessarily say [migration is] a bad thing. I think if there's people who are from different countries who have the right skill set, I don't see why they shouldn't be allowed to work here, because, yeah ... I think it's quite good to have a diverse society, yes. But I guess... I'd want to be welcomed somewhere else to work if I had the same skill set as somebody who lives there. (Lucie,[8] 18 years old)

On the benefit to 'the economy' side, there is a broad theme of migrants putting back more into 'the economy' than they take out. This has many aspects. Some, like Paul,[9] argue free movement is the price to pay for a single market.

> If you're going to be part of the single market then you had to comply with those rules and those rules are to allow free movement of labour from one country to another ... they're bringing more wealth into the country, they are putting more money into the economy than they are taking out.

David is one who sees skilled migration as contributing to the intellectual community and producing economic benefits; he says xenophobia against EU migrants is wrong and that when EU students leave the UK they spread a positive image of the country which ends up benefiting the country economically as well as politically. Joseph has had university lecturers and students from other EU states as lodgers. He says they are 'world-class' intellectuals who should not be shabbily treated. Others who have worked in the university, such as Michael, see migration as essential for what is a growth sector of 'the economy', as well as for any cultural reasons. Fawad has an even more direct economic argument for skilled migration because he manages an electrical exporting company which spends money on UK-based recruitment of engineers but cannot find them, so is forced to recruit from outside. He relishes the multicultural vibrancy of his

---

[8] Lucie does not live in Church district but a similar area.
[9] Paul does not live in Church district but a similar area.

company's staffroom of Germans, Italians and so on. Fawad echoes Alan at the start of this chapter when he talks of how 'lower-grade' work has become more competitive due to migration.

> Where before [a lower-paid job such as working in Costa] was more or less guaranteed, now you need to show, even if you want a job in Costa coffee, you've got to fight for it, you've got to show that you're willing to go that extra mile. But is that a bad thing? If somebody smiles at you and says thank you instead of throwing the coffee at you?

Others recognise the economic benefits of low-skilled workers given the demographics of the UK's ageing population. Referring to the NHS, David asks 'how much can the infrastructure stand if they have to go away again?' Milo,[10] in his twenties, expands on this theme.

> Yes, again, migration often results in growth just as a function of having more increase in the population, often with young workers. And people say that's one of the reasons why Angela Merkel welcomed so many people to Germany, because she needed more labour.

A common refrain overall is that migrants 'bring into the economy more than they take out' (Helen and Jane), 'add to an economy' (Gareth). Phoebe,[11] like many in Church district, refers to some awareness of academic or media research that assesses the overall impact of 'the economy' as positive.

> The economic arguments, I don't fully know them or anything, but [migrants] actually benefit the country in terms of culture and tourism and economic growth.

How 'economic' was your vote in the referendum?

How 'economic' do voters believe their vote in the referendum was? I ask this question towards the end of the interview. I ask it to explore how they understand the term 'economic' rather than as any kind of definitive answer about why they voted. The answers can be put in the context of their previous answers on migration and trade. However, both Hill and Church district participants also sometimes claim one other issue has an 'economic' dimension, and that is sovereignty. These answers highlight interesting issues about how interviewees interpret the term 'economic', which I will explore in greater detail in the next chapter.

---

[10] Milo does not live in Church district but a similar area.
[11] Phoebe does not live in Church district but a similar area.

Hill district

LEAVE VOTERS

When I ask Leavers why they voted to Leave, many answer that in part they wanted the UK to become more independent again, more sovereign. A lot of the commentary on the referendum result suggests opposition to migration for cultural reasons and desire for sovereignty is strongly linked, but many participants believe sovereignty is also linked with 'the economy'.

It is surprising how few interviewees who mention sovereignty as a reason for their referendum vote do so in the narrow sense that it will enable control of migration. Leave voters Gary (in his forties) and Elena (in her thirties) say they are not opposed to migration, and when they say their vote is partly desire for sovereignty, they mean sovereignty in a broad political sense, including control of justice policy.

> For me it was changing EU law. Because I do think there's a lot of things that have happened over X amount of years where we need to do something and they say 'you can't, because you're interfering with blah, blah, blah, blah'.

Those who oppose migration also describe their desire for sovereignty in broad rather than purely 'control of migration' terms.

> And we're supposed to be our own country, England. I know it helps if I do this [makes hand movements on the table] we're here, the [rest of the EU] are over there, we're supposed to govern our own stuff, but we can't do anything. They [the EU] might say, 'oh no, you can't do that, oh no'. We've got to ask them if we can do it … I want us to, all right I want us to run our own place, deal with our own money. I want the government, the law, so that we can have our own law back, not say 'ah, we got to ask somebody else'. Because what's the point in saying Great Britain if we are not really Great, because we are 'yeah we'll do that, but, please sir, can we'? (Beverley, in her sixties)

> [In the EU] certainly everything, including trade things, it was all getting overly discussed by so many other people. I mean how everybody gets a chance just to say their point of view, I mean it could take you months to decide what you're having for tea … It's out of control. (Julie, in her sixties)

Trevor, in his seventies, says migration affected his vote, but '*as well* [my italics] it was them trying to tell us what to do'. Some interviewees who say sovereignty is important explicitly include what political scientists would categorise as the economic issue of the budget. Note that Beverley says 'I want us to … deal with our own money.' Elsewhere she argues we have contributed too much to the EU budget. Steven says 'we send millions out there to Brussels, millions lining their pockets'. Elliott says 'we seem to be paying a hell of a lot of money out to Europe and not seeing much in the way of return'. George says 'We don't control our own money at all and we should be.'

However, not surprisingly perhaps, participants find it hard to characterise how economic their own reasons for voting are. I include an extract from a Hill district focus group to illustrate this.

Interviewer: Thinking back to the referendum, do you think your vote in the referendum was economic? Or was it about other things?

Elliott: I think it was mostly economic because ... we seemed to be, I mean you can only go on what you get from the papers and news on the TV, but we seemed to be the poor relation if you like, at the bottom end of the pile when they're committing these laws and all that.

Beverley: That's a good way of putting it Elliott.

Elliott: They're paying very little back.

George: In my part it was economic, pure and simple. Migration actually played quite a small part in it because although I'm a member of UKIP I only joined UKIP when I realised trade unions were messing up the Labour Party, started looking for another middle-of-the-road party. UKIP is not right-wing and not racist, they're middle-of-the-road.

Interviewer: What was your economic argument then?

George: The fact that we were giving so much money to the EU, not getting it back properly.

Elliott: Like I just said, we are the poor relation.

George: If we said where the money is being spent in this country we would be better off all the way round. The hospitals would be better off, they wouldn't be going privatised the way the Conservative government is making them go, housing would be better, basically if we spent that money ourselves instead of giving it to Europe. We would all be better off; the whole country would be better off ...

Interviewer: [Addressed to Beverley] do you think your referendum vote was quite economic or was there anything else?

Beverley: Yeah and migration.

Elliott: Yeah, well, migration.

In his interview some months before, George had said his Leave vote was 50 per cent 'economic' and 50 per cent 'migration'. Here, several months later in the focus group, George has thought through a position where he clearly and consistently relates his Leave vote to 'the economy' and wants to avoid accusations of racism or xenophobia. But Beverley remains consistent in the focus group, as she had been in her interview, in distinguishing between 'economic' reasons for voting Leave and 'migration' ones.

While Beverley and George differ on '*how* economic', they do seem to have a sense of what they mean by 'economic', including not just trade but also the effects of migration on employment, housing and other resources, and control of the budget as an aspect of sovereignty. Gary, in his forties, also has a clear answer; he says his vote was 50 per cent economic and 50 per cent sovereignty, and argues Brexit will lead to an improvement in the overall economy. He wants Brexit to lead economically to 'something new, something different, something not thought about', which I return to in Chapter 8.

However, other Hill district Leave supporters who mention what most political scientists would categorise as economic arguments against migration do not categorise those arguments as economic. Glenn has included detailed arguments about Eastern European migrants seizing jobs, but when I ask him how economic his vote was, he says 'not at all'. Shelley says her support for Leave was based on 'immigration' and spending on the NHS (the £350-million promise). Despite the content of the rest of her answers on the economic costs of migrants to the benefits bill and increasing unemployment and the fact that there is an economic component to 'the NHS', she still denies that her vote in the referendum had *any* economic element. Neither expressed such strong opposition to migration that their reason for being reluctant could be that their cultural opposition is so much stronger. These responses show people may be unsure generally about how to interpret 'economic', which I return to in the next chapter.

REMAIN VOTERS

There is also a spectrum of beliefs of 'how economic' the vote was for Hill district Remainers. Adam does not interpret 'economic' the way political scientists tend to; he says his reasons for voting Remain were not economic, but the only reasons he does give are the potential damage of Brexit to the car manufacturing industry, which most political scientists would categorise as economic. The rest of the Remainers interpret 'economic' more like a political scientist would and say their reasons were mainly economic. Economics graduate Frances says 'practically all of' her vote was economic; Martin, in his fifties, says yes, 'from an economic point of view, yes, we should have stayed in' and does not offer any other reasons; Rosa, in her forties, says 'an awful lot'. Colin thinks there has been too much migration and that the EU is too large to function but 'economics' tips him to vote to Remain. Lidia is Polish-born and voted to Remain both for political and economic reasons. When they elaborate, they mean economic in the sense of the overall economy, such as GDP levels and trade.

Some argue that their primary reason for voting Remain was not economic. Lucas and Clare, both eighteen, say their main reasons are what could be characterised as self-interested educational. Several have strong political or cultural motivations. Robert, Martha and Ross feel that culturally and politically they are European (and internationalist).

Church district

LEAVE VOTERS

There are only three Leave voters on Hill district. Two vote primarily for cultural reasons, to maintain the UK's Christian heritage, although they also mention economic costs of being in the EU including competition for jobs. In his interview, the third, James, in his seventies, says he voted Leave because:

> The EU is both 'corrupt' and 'undemocratic' and therefore sovereignty is desirable on that basis. (James, in his seventies)

REMAIN VOTERS

Surprisingly, only about half of Remain voters readily acknowledge that their referendum votes were 'mainly' economic. Peter, who is critical of aspects of the EU, is an example of one who voted Remain reluctantly for fear that the economic costs of leaving would be worse than staying in.

> Well that there will be a big hit to the economy of this country [through leaving]. Certainly the way it's being phrased at the moment, leaving the single market and the European Court are retrograde steps and I think they will ... We've already seen the first problem, which is the reduction in the value of sterling.

Rachel has reservations about the cultural and political side of the European Union. She says her vote to Remain was finely balanced; she did it reluctantly and only for 'economic reasons'. Her biggest economic concern was that a lot of 'the City' would move to Frankfurt if the UK voted to leave the European Union and the UK would also be 'thrown into the arms of America' for trade. Others who categorise their Remain vote as 'economic' include Richard, who says 'yes of course ... gosh it was plain as the nose on my face all the economic benefits, not only to me personally, but the country', Gareth ('most of the [reasons]'), Joseph ('a large part of it') and Theresa ('yeah I think it was economic'). When they elaborate, they mean economic in the sense of the overall economy such as GDP levels.

However, a surprising number of Church district Remainers argue that their primary reason was *not* economic. Several have strong political or cultural motivations. Jane says 'I have a gut feeling that I am European', which is echoed by Johnny, Alan, Fawad and Michael. However, even those who say their vote was mainly non-economic acknowledge the *validity* of the economic case. Alan says because he is such a political pro-European, by comparison his economic reasons probably only amount to 25 per cent, 'but that doesn't mean I don't think it's important'. Helen[12] and Phoebe[13] are in a more sceptical position. They say their

[12] Helen does not live in Church district but a similar area.
[13] Phoebe does not live in Church district but a similar area.

reasons for voting Remain were mainly non-economic because the economic reasons could not be assessed; 'how do you know that? How can you predict it? It's never happened before' (Phoebe, eighteen years old).

However, what is also striking about many Church district participants is their common understanding that 'other *less-educated* people' voted Leave because they were anti-migration. Hill district's Lidia, a nurse originally from Poland, makes this distinction.

> There were some comments, especially in the hospital. I can really see that clearly, because we've got different levels of people working, and, if you go to more educated, there's less talk about Brexit and all that. If you go a bit lower, like cleaners, they like to talk about it. And as soon as it all happened they started saying to the young nurses from Poland or any other countries 'are you packing your luggages now?' [Laughs] ... Like they said, it was open season. Yeah, they call it that way in a bad way when somebody died and somebody was killed, but in the soft way, the way people spoke, some people, I didn't even think that they were going to turn so quickly and they were going to show their real face after Brexit happened. (Lidia, in her forties)

The fourteen participants mentioning that 'other' less-educated people voted Leave for 'false' anti-migration reasons in their interviews are all from occupational groups B and C. Alan (in his forties) says 'the less-educated bulk of the people' are anti-immigration. Alice (in her seventies) talks of 'the ordinary people, the less educated ... all went for Brexit because of the migrants'. Fawad (in his forties) says 'it was a total immigration vote, nothing more'. Frances (in her seventies), who lives in an area with a lot of Leave voters, says:

> They say they all have ... a friend of a friend of a friend whose brother has a friend who knows that the council are letting houses to immigrants ... it's all nonsense ... because they're xenophobic to start with.

They did not 'understand' the different types of migrant (Theresa,[14] in her fifties).

Peter, Rachel and Rebecca are high-income participants who are more sympathetic to low-income people's anti-migration beliefs, perceiving it as in part due to justified economic concerns about pay and job security. They believe 'the economy' generally has benefited from migration but that any price for that has been borne disproportionately by lower-income groups. Joseph says:

> I understand how people could feel in certain areas if they've got sort of bottom-of-the-pyramid-type jobs and they see people who come, these people who come are

[14] Theresa does not live in Church district but a similar area.

smarter than they are and they can do the job … I think that was the whole point about the Brexit ideas and that's very, very sad.

An added element is that these 'other' or 'less-educated' people did not understand the economic arguments, and by implication did not care about 'the economy'. Lidia comments that people did not understand the economic arguments about the benefits of the EU. Richard (in his eighties) says 'they didn't realise … the immense amount of benefit we receive from the European Union economic community'. Fawad echoes this point: 'people didn't understand the economy and the guys who try to explain it did it very badly'. In David's view, lower-income voters who voted Leave tend to read the *Sun* and their referendum concerns, 'about immigrants swamping the country and getting our sovereignty back', are what he defines as populist. He argues 'these phrases … are very attractive because they resonate with something, but [they] didn't have the word economy anywhere in them'.

Conclusion

This chapter reveals some complex reasoning. I conclude on trade first. Across both districts understanding of trade is sketchy, almost disinterested, whether participants are Remainers or Leavers. There is no noticeable increase in depth of understanding in the later interviews as news coverage of trade negotiations intensified during 2017 and 2018. This finding raises the possibility that everyday actors feel more connected to some features of 'the economy' than others. It shows that even high-income participants who say they follow other aspects of 'the economy', unless they are directly involved with trade through their jobs, have less self-interest in following this aspect than they do inflation or interest rates. Their greater tendency to accept the Remain arguments about trade may be a question of trust in experts rather than their own reasoning. Also across both districts, there is a subsidiary pattern of those who voted Leave having faith in trade deals with the Commonwealth. However, even this talk of the Commonwealth is sketchy and not well developed.

Second, I conclude on migration. I argued there is much controversy over this in the political science literature I reviewed in Chapter 1 where some scholars (Inglehart and Norris 2016, 2019) categorise opposition to immigration as 'cultural'. How much is opposition to migration in Hill district an economic issue? These findings reveal it is for two reasons. First, some scholars have argued that respondents may exaggerate their economic arguments against migration because they know the cultural ones are less acceptable (McLaren and Johnson 2007; Kaufmann 2018). This may be the case for a few participants here, but older participants in this study who do oppose migration for cultural reasons, such as Beverley, feel free to express that cultural opposition. And some who express economic opposition are from migration or minority ethnic backgrounds themselves or do not, in what are lengthy interviews, show any signs of cultural opposition. Second, the depth of participants' economic arguments against migration is striking. In some cases it is based on misinformation, such as in the draining effect on the exchequer, where there is some consensus by economists that migration makes a net contribution (Dustmann and Frattini 2014). However, participants argue that even if migrants pay more in tax than they take out in benefits, they still should not receive as much as they do in benefits. Some economists would agree with participants' reasoning that migration depresses *unskilled* wage rates (Dustmann et al. 2008; Nickell and Saleheen 2015), although the overwhelming consensus among economists is that migration benefits wages overall through economic growth.

How do the strong arguments in Hill district against migration on economic grounds compare with Church district? In Church district there is a similar age divide as in Hill district of older participants being more opposed to migration, and some of them are opposed for cultural reasons. However, generally, 'anti-migration' participants in Church district appear more 'detached' than in Hill district. They are not in competition with migrants for jobs or resources and do not make the same economic arguments against migration.

Is being in favour of migration an economic issue? In Church district some pro-migration participants are self-interested in their support for migration because they say they benefit directly from free movement. Church district participants are more likely to acknowledge the benefits of migration to 'the economy' overall, such as to GDP. Particularly in Church district, there is a perception that 'other, less-educated' people voted to Leave for anti-migration reasons and because they did not understand the economic arguments. In both districts the young seem to be in favour of migration either for both economic and cultural reasons or, more simply, because they just do not see it as an issue.

Third, how do participants approach evaluating whether their referendum votes were 'economic'? In Church district, surprisingly, at least half of Remain voters argue 'the economy' was not their primary motivation and some even express scepticism about some of the economic forecasting. Many of them effectively have cultural reasons for their Remain vote. In Hill district, some Remainers, such as Rosa, say their reasoning was in part economic. Ruby, Andy and Colin, for instance, all voted reluctantly to Remain for the sake of 'the economy' even though they were opposed to migration. These participants tend to be using 'economic' in the way many political behaviour writers would, in terms of overall GDP.

For Leave voters, the evaluation of how economic their votes were is more complex. In Hill district, some are inconsistent about the economic reasons they give, or do not categorise what most political scientists would say are economic reasons as economic. I explore further in the next chapter whether there is a reluctance to use the term. However, while not many Leave voters argue that leaving will benefit 'the economy' in the sense of increasing trade and GDP, instead emphasising we will not be damaged by leaving as much as official forecasters predict, they do attach weight to other economic benefits of 'taking back control'. They care deeply about regaining sovereignty. Sovereignty is not just about controlling migration but far more all-encompassing as a concept, including an economic element of saving the budget contribution and spending it more wisely and effectively at home. The three Church district Leave voters do not emphasise the economic benefits of regaining control of the budget as much as those in Hill district; one is more concerned about being shackled to a 'failing' EU and the democratic side of sovereignty and the other two are culturally opposed to the EU as a project.

Generally across both districts, there is not a clear-cut divide of Remain voters saying their vote was economic and Leave voters saying it was not. This runs counter to the results of the 'what is the most important issue in deciding how to vote' polls conducted just before the referendum that I mentioned in Chapter 1, which showed huge majorities of those saying 'economy' intended to vote Remain. It suggests the real picture is both more nuanced and complex. This chapter raises questions about how participants define 'the economy' and economic, which is the subject of the next chapter.

Finally, this chapter raises questions about who the 'Other' is. There is much mention of 'othering' in the political science literature. However, this chapter reveals that while 'othering' of migrants is a consistent theme, there may also be othering of 'older', 'less-educated' or even more educated in the case of 'expert' people.

6

'The word economy is hollow'

Rosa is in her late forties and was brought up in (low-income) Hill district near the school where she now works. She is deeply attached to it and volunteers in the local neighbourhood centre, but, like most people her age on the estate, when she left home she could only get housing on the outskirts of the city. As well as the school, she has also worked in factories and as a telephonist and brought up a son, partly reliant on in-work benefits. I ask her how she defines the term 'the economy' and she laughs.

> Economy now? Bottomless pit. Rip-off Britain. I think the economy is built on being ripped off actually ... The trickle-down effect of the economy; I've seen little cartoony videos of that. I've said 'oh yes, definitely get that!' And at the start of the recession they say 'oh we'll have to be in a recession because we can't afford the national health system, but, hey, let's throw a few billion pounds into the stock market so the rich don't get poorer, and we'll just take all the money from the poor and let them be poorer'. I do feel that has been done in the last few years, big time.

Rosa is articulate and political. She talks fast, expressing an underlying anger that alternates with despair. The other Hill district participants I interview are sometimes less confident, but many of them share her perception of 'the economy' as rigged, where 'the rich write the rules' (Misha, in her thirties). In contrast, (high-income) Church district's Michael talks about 'the economy' in more benign terms.

> I'm also very conscious that ... the economy is very important. It matters a lot in our lives in all sorts of ways. Healthcare, social care and education and so on. And therefore I understand that what happens in this country, particularly to our young people, depends on whether we have a strong economy.

'The economy' is hard to define; as David comments, 'the word in itself is rather hollow'. In this chapter, I first demonstrate how participants 'define' 'the economy'. Then, taking all their interview and focus groups answers into account, I explore first Church district and then Hill district participants' understanding of 'the economy'.

Thin definitions

In Chapter 1 I mentioned that Economy.org (Norrish 2017) asked respondents in an online poll for an open-ended 'definition' of 'economy' and answers were quite thin. I get similarly thin responses. When I ask participants to define 'the economy' and 'economic', most of them pause, sigh or grimace.[1] Participants find it difficult to go into any depth or be precise about what 'the economy' is. I group their responses into six, giving the district they come from in brackets.

The first three groups define 'the economy' and 'economic' as general umbrella terms, similar to the neoclassical understanding I outlined in Chapter 1.

> I suppose it's the process of making money, that's the way I would look at it. The way of doing business and making money in our world. (Alan, in his forties, Church district)

> The economy relates to tangible wealth, money or properties or something. (David, in his seventies, Church district)

> It's just the way the economy is working, it's how everything sort of fits together. (Robert, in his fifties, Hill district)

> Stuff relating to the economy, jobs, GDP, trade – whatever. (Lachlan, in his twenties, Hill district)

> If you say the economy and economic matters, well I suppose I think it is being about money, finance, the broad world of business. (Michael, in his seventies, Church district)

> To do with finances and stuff like that, whether you're in profit or loss and things like export imports, so basically the implication on all of us. (Julie, in her sixties, Hill district)

The second group focuses on it being more about money or finance.

> Finances and money. (Elena, in her thirties, Hill district)

> I guess just how money works. (Clare,[2] eighteen years old)

> Money and stuff. (Howard,[3] eighteen years old)

> The state of how the country's in financially. (Shelley, in her fifties, Hill district)

> Money, finance, banks, government, the Treasury. (Gareth, in his forties, Hill district)

---

[1] It does not make much difference whether the question is phrased 'how do you define 'economic'? or 'how do you define the economy?' In some interviews, when participants feel uneasy that they will be put on the spot, I find that phrasing the question as understanding of the term 'economic' generates *fuller* responses than phrasing it about 'the economy'. I can then follow up with questions about what their gut reaction is on hearing the word 'economy'. But phrasing does not affect the thrust of the answers.

[2] Clare does not live in Hill district but a similar area.

[3] Howard does not live in Hill district but a similar area.

Isn't it like around money and if it's, if there's a lot or not like companies, I don't know. (Maxine,[4] eighteen years old)

Money stuff, yeah [laughs] business and money sort of thing, but yeah. (Lisa,[5] eighteen years old)

How people make and use money. (Jane, in her seventies, Church district)

Probably something to do with kind of money and the growth of money in society. The economy links in with business as well. (Lucie,[6] eighteen years old)

Yes [Pause]. That's a really hard question. I suppose I define it as the sum of all the wealth that's generated and lost, something like that [laughs]. (Ross, in his thirties, Hill district)

A third group, again from both districts, emphasise the government in some way in their definitions.

The handling of the state's finances, I suppose, policies for how you fit into the world. (Joseph, in his seventies, Church district)

What the government's money is spent on? (Mary, in her seventies, Church district)

Oh, everything to do with money and the government and all that jazz. (Alice, in her seventies, Church district)

Is it about money and how government, for example, spends money? But I have no clue, to be honest. (Amelia, in her twenties, Hill district)

That's usually the state of the finances of the country or the local council or whatever. (Colin, in his sixties, Hill district)

A fourth group, who are all women, brings in the micro or household level.

Oh god, for me [economy would be] just if we could manage it ourselves as a family, you know, and yeah, I think it's just the everyday cost of living. (Ruby, in her fifties, Hill district)

Well I would pluck out words that I don't really understand, but that's what I would do, so I would say I know that there's a micro level and a macro level. (Rachel, in her fifties, Church district)

I think there's two things. There's kinda, if you like, the big picture economy, macro level whatever. Apart from, I think of it myself on a more personal level, you know the household economy, live within my means and stuff. (Helen,[7] in her forties, high-income participant but outside of Church district)

I suppose it's to do with the flow of money, the monetary situation, whether it's micro or macro scale. (Stephanie, in her fifties, Church district)

[4] Maxine does not live in Hill district but a similar area.
[5] Lisa does not live in Hill district but a similar area.
[6] Lucie does not live in Church district but a similar area.
[7] Helen does not live in Church district but a similar area.

I was thinking very much of our family and the money coming into our family in different ways and how it's then spent and what it is at the end. It is like that, but it's not like that, because it's hundreds, thousands and millions of times more complex than that. (Rebecca, in her fifties, Church district focus group)

Some eighteen-year-old sixth-form college students perceive the question as relating to Economics as an academic subject, perhaps to justify why they find the question hard to answer.

Money [laughs], global stuff I guess, international relations, that sort of thing. It's a bit daunting as well because I wouldn't be able to define it, probably because it encompasses so many different things. It's quite, you think of it as quite an adult, grown-up phrase. I don't know, it's like I did History at A-level last year. We did financial, social, political and economic and I was always focused on the political and social stuff. The economic was 'oh it's numbers'. It's a bit harder to grasp maybe. (Phoebe,[8] 18 years old)

I don't really do economics. (Howard,[9] 18 years old)

A final group, mainly from Hill district, define the economy as about efficiency, saving or cost of living.

You have to be careful what you are doing, you know, you must remember that you have to have the rent paid each week, my insurance has to be paid each week, you know, you have to be careful what you do with money, you know. (Jean, in her seventies, Hill district)

I don't know what the word is, economic, economical, you got to look at things and draw in a bit I suppose. Economical, that's what I would say, they're spending thousands or millions and we can't afford it … just save it for when, then we can go from there. (Steven, in his eighties, Hill district)

Well I've not really thought a lot about it, to be quite honest. Just like, its economical to do so and so. (Trevor, in his seventies, Hill district)

Prices. (Chris, in his sixties, Hill district)

Some say something broader. For Gary, in his forties in Hill district, 'economic' is 'stability, the value of something, that's how I would define it. Yeah'. For Misha, in Hill district in her thirties, the economy is 'the savings but also civility'.

Questions asking participants to 'define the economy' do not immediately reveal deep insights. So many participants have a default position of 'money, finances' that it is hard to extract much significance from the first three groups of definitions. It may be significant that the micro/macro distinction is raised by women. It may also be significant that the last group, all from Hill district, are furthest away from the neoclassical understanding of 'the economy' as an

---

[8] Phoebe does not live in Church district but a similar area.
[9] Howard does not live in Hill district but a similar area.

umbrella term, seeing 'the economy' instead as to do with efficiency or prices. The rest of the chapter contextualises these answers, drawing on the rest of their talk and the focus groups, to develop deeper insights.

Church district

'The economy' as umbrella or 'ship of state'

Church district participants share that aspect of the neoclassical understanding of 'the economy' I outlined in Chapter 1: that it is a neutral and umbrella term for interconnected forces.

In Chapter 1 I introduced Rachel, who had a frugal upbringing and was still frugal, although she also speculates in shares. Rachel participated in movements of monetary forces beyond her household. Some other Church district participants are directly involved in 'the economy' as private-sector workers and entrepreneurs. There is a particular *intensity* to the comments of those currently working in the private sector. Alan demonstrates that even though he is also interested in politics, he has to follow 'the economy' closely to assess how general economic conditions like the level of employment or interest rates will affect his property business. Throughout his interview he acknowledges how one aspect of 'the economy' can impact on another. One of his examples is:

> It's important inflation is controlled to a certain level. We certainly don't want deflation. If you've got deflation, people put off spending until next month and that can send the economy spinning downwards. (Alan)

Fawad, who says knowing about 'the economy' is a professional requirement for his job in manufacturing exports, is particularly anxious when contemplating the effects of Brexit and trade negotiations. He says:

> So I'm scared a little bit what's going to happen in the next couple of years, because we are a fit strong economy, but for how long? (Fawad)

However, the difference between Church district participants working in the private sector compared with those in the public sector or retired is in intensity of feeling rather than understanding of 'the economy'. Those who work in the public sector or are now retired from it also frame a lot of their answers in both interviews and focus groups around a common assumption that there is such a thing as 'the economy' and that it affects everyone.

I take out the interviewer's words from interview transcripts and then conduct an NVivo word frequency search for participants' use of the word 'economy'. All 24 occupational group A/B participants, 40 per cent of all participants, make 145 references to 'the economy' compared with the 36 CDE participants, 60 per cent of the total, who make only 77 references. *Participants from occupational groups A/B are therefore more than three times more likely to use the term 'economy' in talk about 'the economy' than those from C1, C2, D or E.* They appear to be at ease with and comfortable about using 'the economy' as a term.

Most Church district participants are *positive* about 'the economy'. Many older participants recognise they have 'lived through a golden age' (James) because of the benefits 'the economy' has brought them in terms of job and housing opportunities. I characterise Church district participants as cheerleaders because, from the sidelines, they hope 'the economy' will do well. Michael, who has worked all his life in an academic environment, eschewing a higher-paid career in business for what interests him and the greater security, still says, as I highlighted with his words at the head of the chapter, that a strong economy is 'important'. Retired teacher Richard takes this support for 'the economy' further with an analogy of the ship as an economy and a sense of 'the economy' as national. For him 'the economy' is:

> The national state of play, largely. I think of what happened in 2008 the crash, you know, that affected everybody and everybody's form of employment or their living was affected … Everybody became very aware at that stage that the national economy was terribly important.

> I keep an eye on the economy, I'm interested in, as I said before, the movement. Some industries have flourished, some have sunk without trace and it's very sad for those people.

> If I was a younger man I'd be terribly interested how the ship of state was going to fare you know, and, you know, I'd hate to see us go down or have serious difficulties.

The sense of the cheerleader who wants to hear good news is evident in Harry's comment. Wishing in some ways that he had gone into business rather than the auditing side of the health service, he says about the economic news: 'I think it's very interesting and I like to hear success, I want to hear success for everyone's sake'.

Most Church district participants therefore say they are *interested* in 'the economy'. I ask participants whether they follow the news and economic news in particular, including what their gut reaction is when the 'economic news' comes on. I categorise sixteen of the twenty-three Church district residents as regular news users[10] and eleven of the seventeen participants who say they are interested in the economic news come from Church district. However, it is surprising that some who say they follow the news, listening to it and reading newspapers regularly, are unaware that the government is in debt and are sketchy on trade issues, so the self-categorisation of 'interested in the news' may in some cases just reflect a desire to appear interested and a good citizen and to trust in expertise, which I return to later in this chapter.

---

[10] The category of regular news users includes those who say they consume print or online/broadcast new sources 'regularly'.

Some participants say they find aspects of economic news hard to understand, but they still make an effort to follow 'the economy'. In some cases they are interested because they have shares. However, Michael does not have shares but still follows up his belief in the importance of 'the economy' with close attention to its progress.

> I try to get my head round the question, is the UK currently doing well or not? And that is closely related to analysing what the significance is of the fact that the pound is sinking like a stone and the FTSE 100 is in the stratosphere.

Rebecca, who follows politics less closely than Michael, finds 'the economy' even harder to understand, but still says, about the 'economic news' coming on:

> I wouldn't think, 'oh whoopee'! If it was education or health I might be more interested than if they're talking about the economy, but I know that it is really important because it's the bedrock of everything else. I mean, basically, if the economy isn't doing very well then we haven't got any more money to spend on hospitals or schools.

Church district participants' frequent and familiar use of the term 'economy' implies they identify with it in some way. They appear to share an understanding of 'the economy' as an umbrella term for interconnected monetary, financial or business-related forces or activity. Despite the comments of Richard about 'the national economy', many also highlight the effects of global forces on 'the national economy' (Fawad, Alan, Joseph, Rachel, Michael, Peter, Paul, Helen).

Impersonal forces and unease about how they are steered

In comparison with Hill district participants in later sections of this chapter, on the whole, Church district participants also seem to accept the aspect of the neoclassical understanding that economic forces are impersonal. This comes through even as they complain that governments have not done more to steer the impersonal forces in recent decades. In this section I explore this aspect of their understanding.

A few Church district participants could be described as anti-materialist and have reservations about an 'economy' divorced from social goals. They have chosen careers with lower salaries and want to live their lives according to faith or environmental ethics. Helen, trained as an accountant, is less concerned with money as she gets older and her faith becomes more important to her. She says growth-based economies are not 'realistic'.

> I think we need to build an economy that is sustainable, low-growth or whatever, and try to build up people's lives and look at this quality-of-life issue. (Helen[11])

---

[11] Helen does not live in Church district but a similar area.

Most Church district participants express less deep-rooted reservations about 'the economy' than Helen, but are critical of the way it has been steered in recent years. In previous chapters, some Church district participants are uneasy about the slow recovery since 2008. They do not believe they have suffered personally, but are concerned about the growing strains on low-income workers. Similarly, when discussing 'the economy' more generally, while a few Church district participants want 'the economy' to be subject primarily to market forces because that will result in optimal growth, the majority are uneasy because they believe economic needs have become too disconnected from social ones.

What does the unease consist of? Some believe there has been too much of the wrong kind of government intervention, skewed towards big business as in the case of the bank bailout. Alan is one example of a participant who not only describes themselves as a free marketeer and economically liberal, in favour of free movement and trade, but also believes that government should act to pre-vent abuses of the market. The post-2008 bank bailout was an unfair use of taxpayers' money. Instead, government should have briefly nationalised banks, imposed conditions and tighter regulation, including promoting competition and preventing cartels. He also asks 'why are we paying people [top bankers] so much? I don't know the answer but do accept it's not right as it is.'

Others believe government should intervene more broadly for the sake of social aims. The difference between those who accept 'the economy' can and should be separate from society and those who do not comes out most clearly in a focus group exchange between Jane and James. Jane has worked all her life as a healthcare professional, follows politics closely and describes herself as having centrist political views. She starts with a definition of 'the economy'.

> I think of the economy as a mixture of things, the balance of what's going into the country's coffers and what they're spending and how that is influenced by the current world situation, the state of those factors which are producing income such as the manufacturing industry et cetera. All the things that are producing income balanced against all the things that are taking money out of the public purse, such as the number of people needing benefits and the demography of the country, such as the ageing population, the number of unemployed and so on. It's a sort of dynamic situation with all those factors.

She acknowledges the 'current world situation' and 'the factors which are produc-ing income', but her definition, focusing on 'coffers' and 'the public purse', is quite government- or public sector-orientated. James says:

> You're thinking the economy is only government. The economy is the sum of all activities that take place.

Jane then characterises taxation receipts as 'credits' because they can be spent on goods such as the health service. However, she is picked up on this by James, who argues that taxation can detract from 'the economy'.

> You could argue it's taking money out of the pot. Taxation is a zero-sum game. The country takes money from me so I lose ... taxation is moving money around inside the economy, the more I'm taxed the less economic activity I can undertake and the only way for the government to undertake activity is to raise taxes.

James is one of the few to express support for the discipline of economics, arguing:

> I would say I'm reasonably positive about [economics]. I think there are some aspects of economics as a subject that can tell us some things we need to know.

He says he understands what one of the other participants depicts as the neo-classical economics representation of 'the economy' as a 'black box ... a machine that generates cash' (Peter), where a polluting employer can be perceived as contributing to 'the economy'. Both Peter and James have studied economics in some form and show by their other comments that they understand, even if they do not always agree with, some of the tenets economists hold. However, Jane counters with:

> That is your way of looking at it [the economy], that's the way you look at it. But I'm looking at it in a different way ... I'm looking at the economy as a central thing which is serving the country as a whole, and taxation is where the money gets put into that central pot ... I'm trying to say for me the economy is, your household economy is, the way you balance your books. And the amount of tax you pay is clearly something that is on the debit side, but if you look at the economy of the nation as a whole, there's a lot of money going in a lot of money coming out and that is dependent, what's going in is dependent on the activities of all the *people* [her emphasis] in that nation ... Taxation for me is on the credit side in that big picture. That's the way I look at it and obviously the purpose of this research project is to look at the way different people are looking at the economy, so we clearly are looking at it slightly differently. (Jane)

She is backed by David, who believes there may be a psychological element to people developing different mindsets, which make them support, for instance, a more planned economy versus a more market-based one. At one stage he says that 'as a human', rights and poverty matter. He finds the concept of a disembedded economy hard to comprehend. He does not understand how there can appear to be a mismatch between people's wellbeing and perceptions of the health of economies.

> In Italy for years, I get the impression that they just ran up a bigger and bigger deficit but nobody seemed to mind and everybody did all right. What's the economy of that country? Is it what happens to individuals, because they seem to be doing

all right, or is it the debt that the country is running up that means one day, like Greece, it will implode?

Peter articulates the basis for his case that the UK should adopt a more neo-Keynesian policy that supports social goals like employment and greater social equality. He says:

> A number of American economists are famous for saying this: 'there is only money and in the end everything reduces to money and if you can make a profit out of it then great'. But I think in other societies, and I would hope that Britain's still one of those, we have a slightly different view, that it's the welfare, the happiness, the standard of living, the quality of life, the respect for the environment, things of that kind that are also important and should also be taken into account. But because they're traditionally not counted as monetary things, they're dismissed by economists who then have other policies which may well maximise profits or wealth or income or benefit certain groups, but not to the benefit of the country as a whole.

Hill district

Less of an umbrella: 'the economy' and 'my economy'

Hill district participants talk in depth about the eight aspects of 'the economy' I ask about in interviews and are voluble on how they manage financially and about the narrative of their economic lives. However, they are three times *less* likely than Church district participants to mention 'the economy' in their interviews. The gap between real economic lives and the abstract or official 'economy' is epitomised by Jean, who lives off the state pension without getting into debt and budgets efficiently and creatively for her and her family. I ask 'how much do you think you know about "the economy"?' She answers:

> I don't know a lot about *the* economy really [her emphasis]. [Turns to husband] Do you? [No, no].

When I comment to Gary that he seems to understand a lot about 'the economy', he says:

> I think I know about *my* economy and what relates to me. But for somebody else it might be a totally different thing, the way it relates to them [his emphasis].

Gary implies that he has a sense of his economy and the things that affect it, which will be different for others. He is clear by his tone, however, that I am wrong in my assessment that he understands '*the* economy'. For him, 'my economy' and 'the economy' are distinct. In the first section of this chapter I noted that some Hill district residents define 'economy' as 'efficiency' or saving; eighteen-year-old Clare highlights how people may not always associate the two as being part of the same phenomenon. She says while 'talking about money and things', her everyday economy, 'you don't necessarily think, "oh yes, this is the economy"!' However, even those in Hill district mentioned at the start of the chapter who initially define 'the economy' broadly along the lines of the neoclassical definition of it as an umbrella term for forces, reveal in subsequent comments their divergence from the Church district understanding.

The first difference is that low-income participants tend to see 'the economy' less as an 'umbrella', in the sense that their economic lives interact with 'the economy' at fewer points than those from the higher-income district. Linda, who is a carer living on benefits, spells out that she has not been on holiday abroad, cannot borrow from a bank and does not have savings or a mortgage. While 'the economy' impacts on her family's employment, she is less self-interested in interest rates and exchange rates than higher-income participants.

'The economy' being less like an umbrella links with a sense of being less connected to it than in Church district. It comes out in this comparison between two focus group exchanges. When I ask 'do you feel connected to or close to the economy?' participants in the Church district focus group respond that they are 'part of it' (James), still 'involved', even though lacking 'control' (Peter). In contrast, the same question gets a far more 'disconnected' response in a Hill district focus group.

> **Misha:** So I don't feel connected to it; I feel like I'm a … victim of circumstances of the economy so I feel like I just have to sit back and take it like … if taxes are being raised.
> **Shelley:** Yeah because there's nothing we can do. We're not powerful enough to be able to do anything about it anyway … we've just got to get on with things.
> **Linda:** Accept what the rich dish out to us … If you're just a regular person they don't hear it because you're nothing to it, you're not going to contribute or give nothing.

The crucial point Linda makes is both that they contribute less and are less connected. On the point of whether 'the economy' affects them, some members of that focus group later argue that because they have no savings they will not be affected and that 'the economy' does not 'affect us like it affects the rich'.

Robert describes an aspect of distance between everyday and official economies. He hints at how alienated 'average' figures make lower-income people feel. The sentiment behind what he says is that many people feel distant from generalised statements and national indicators.

> I don't think [the experts] actually probably see things from the grassroots. They commentate on the City's view and the City's view is, nine times out of ten, not what somebody who is at the coalface, how they see it. They don't see it like the price of milk going up or the price of bread or anything like that, they just see it as

'oh yeah, the average wage in this country is £25,000'. Yes maybe, but in reality in [our city] it's not. And I think they generalise too much.

When Hill district participants mention the broader economy beyond theirs, they differ from Church district participants in portraying it as less benign. They are more likely to believe either that 'the economy' at best will not affect them positively or at worst will affect them negatively compared with Church district participants. 'The economy' is for the benefit of others. For Martin 'the economy' is a negative term because of inequality.

> [The economy is] good, bad and indifferent [laughs]. I think it varies. It depends how you look at it. You look at some people and you just wonder how they survive. They are living literally every day wondering where their next penny is coming from. And then you look at another side of people and they haven't got a care in the world. They probably wouldn't even know how much money they've got in the bank.

Linda interprets the eight aspects of 'the economy' featured on the interview prompt cards (debt, government spending, taxation, employment, trade, migration, inflation, banks) as depressingly negative phenomena.

> What I've told you about banks … it's the same as really with the debt thing, banks come in … it's all the same circle, all your little things you've got [the eight cards], that is a circle and there is a little human being in the middle of that circle and, bit by bit, he hits every single level of what you've said. You know, he goes through that in his lifetime and he experiences every single bit, every word there [on the cards] he'll experience, and it's just so sad.

Hill district participants are less interested in the economic news than Church district ones. An illustration of this is in an exchange between Misha (in her thirties) and Shelley (in her fifties). In lengthy interviews and focus groups where there is open and wide-ranging discussion, Misha, child of a Jamaican father, does not show evidence of any cultural opposition to migration. However, both participants previously expressed beliefs that many migrants receive benefits, although they also ridicule those who exaggerated the scale of that. In this exchange, Misha is trying to convince Shelley to let migrants in who are fleeing persecution but never once mentions official statistics that show their contribution to the exchequer is net positive.

Shelley: I do believe it's a bit out of control, the immigration.

Misha: But then if it was the other way around, wouldn't you want someone to let you in? Doesn't hate just breed hate?

Shelley: But we're only one little country … and the more we just let in, I totally get like why they want to come here, but the more people we let in, we've got to pay for every single person, so that's going to affect *our* economy [her emphasis].

Misha: [If World War III happened] I would want someone to let me in … I can only imagine what those families are going through over there. Shouldn't we be that country to be like 'come, we'll offer you refuge, come'.

Shelley: But it does affect our economy.

Misha: Isn't that worth it? As a Christian I'd want to say 'I'd rather we all share one loaf of bread together' …

Shelley: It's the fear that they put out about how much it would cost us to have these immigrants here, how much it affects our economy.

Misha tells me elsewhere she mainly relies on social media for news, which is like 'Chinese whispers'. Therefore the strongest explanation, at least in her case, is not that she *rejects* the official statistics on the positives of migration to the exchequer, but that she has not *heard* them.

Some argue economic news is depressing. Elena, in her thirties, finds the economic news depressing because of how cuts may affect her.

Yeah it's always full of dread isn't it? 'What are they planning now, oh no, who's it going to hit first?'

Hearing the national economic indicators reinforces feelings of how far one is from the 'average' wage or house price. Rosa is a highly political teaching assistant in her forties who volunteers at a community centre, but she nevertheless comments in a despairing way about whether she should follow the economic news.

Is there any advantage in knowing any more than you already know? When you don't earn much you haven't got much to count. You don't even need Maths! [Laughs]. Oh, I don't know.

Some say they make an attempt to understand economic issues only on a 'need-to-know' basis. Some Church district participants also articulate this view. For example, Rebecca says she makes an effort to follow 'the economy' 'on a need-to-know basis; it's where it affects you, it's where it impacts on your life'. However, she was in a minority. In Hill district, 'need-to-know' is more common and deeply rooted. Hill district's Diane illustrates 'need-to-know' when she elaborates on how she tries not to learn about benefit changes, unless they are the in-work ones that will affect her, in part because she works so hard she cannot spare the effort.

So until you're affected by it I don't think you really going to understand it. Yeah, that's really all about all … if I've got a real good focus on it then I get my claws into it, but until it's affected you then I don't think … Like with benefit cutbacks and things, it didn't really apply to us. We've got people talking about it, like it's going on to universal credit so we were told today, but we don't claim [universal credit], so we don't need to know. Unless we need to know we're not really into it all.

Despite 'need-to-know', many Hill district participants do have a sense of 'the economy' beyond their local economy. For instance, Shelley says:

> It's a domino effect. If someone hasn't got money to spend, money on getting their hair done, that affects that business, that business is not buying the products and that affects that business. It's then like a domino effect.

'The rich write the rules'

When directly asked to define 'the economy' most low-income participants, such as Elena, give similar answers to high-income participants, that it is to do with 'finances and money'. Such answers imply they share high-income participants' understanding of 'the economy' as an umbrella term for impersonal forces. However, whereas in the rest of their interviews and focus groups high-income participants flesh out the definition in ways that support the original perception of impersonal forces, low-income participants reveal a different understanding, such as when Linda says:

> I think it's about the rich getting richer and the poor getting poorer [laughs]. That's how I see the economy.

Andy (in his sixties) says:

> Unfortunately [the economy is] the working-class people that tend to suffer and, dare I say it to cliché it, the rich get richer … when it comes to managing to live I've seen people in this area with children going around with ragged clothes, which even in this day and age is ridiculous. And you see people in their ivory towers and their mansions and their stupidly big parties.

Rosa perceives 'the economy' as a whole and is one of those who mention it often, and as I showed at the start of this chapter, she elaborates on a feature of it as rigged against people like her. As well as believing 'the economy' 'rips people off' she believes it represents itself falsely and is a 'ruse' because in fact the real work is done by 'grafters' who do not see the benefits.

> Umm, I would watch it [the economic news], obviously, because I am interested in the pound and how it's depreciating and what you can't buy with it anymore and things like that, but not really interested in the stock markets and what's going up and what's going down because, again, it's like a ruse as it were. 'Oh we'll show you', but actually that ain't what it's really built, based, on. It's built on graft, isn't it? Someone, somewhere, is grafting for those peaks and it ain't the managers. But I watch it because actually it's best to know than not to know even if you don't like what you know, or see. I don't really believe any of it to be perfectly honest, but you've got to see it to not believe it.

Linda says we 'accept what the rich dish out'. In another focus group of older low-income participants, Elliott and George make the same kind of comment to Beverley when she says she wants the government to spend her taxes where she wants.

Elliott: But they don't.
George: No, they don't. They spend it where they're looking after their rich friends.
Elliott: Where it suits them, look after themselves and then you're left with whatever is left down the line.

Many in Hill district believe the rich write the rules in 'the economy'. Linda says 'I think money talks, that's a simple fact of life …' Julie, a retired clerical worker, says, to add to her definition of 'the economy', that 'the bank thing's economic, all those years ago'. But she adds that, despite the 'economic wrongdoing', banks were not punished. A focus group of low-income participants takes it for granted that the rich write the rules.

Shelley: [The rich] are always looking at 'right, we want to keep our riches so we will make this rule, we'll make that rule'.
Linda: Nobody ever wants to lose their money.
Misha: Majority of [the rich] are like 'what about my money? I inherited all my money and I want to keep it all …'
Linda: 'My parents worked hard for that' [laughs].
Misha: 'How can me and my friends keep it all?'

To recap, the four differences in interpretation of 'the economy' between high- and low-income participants are that, for the latter, it is less of an umbrella term, more negative and depressing, exerts more power over them and the rich write the rules for it. I argue that a term that encapsulates these is 'rigged'.

I explore 'rigged' in more depth. Low-income participants may see 'the economy' as negative and not benefiting them and they also have less of a perception of it as 'impersonal' than high-income participants because they believe powerful people play such a significant role in manipulating it. I counted in NVivo across all of the interview and focus group transcripts of over sixty hours of talk about 'the economy' for references to social groups including the terms 'rich', 'poor', 'better off', 'worse off', 'high income', 'low income', 'middle class' and 'working class'. Figure 6.1 illustrates that low-income participants make many more references to social groups in their talk than high-income ones.[12] This finding may reflect how much low-income participants believe rich and powerful people play a part in 'the economy', reinforcing their sense of it as rigged. I suggest they therefore see 'the economy' as both less neutral and 'impersonal' than higher-income groups.

---

[12] Occupational group C, D and E participants do make up a larger proportion of the sample as a whole: 60 per cent.

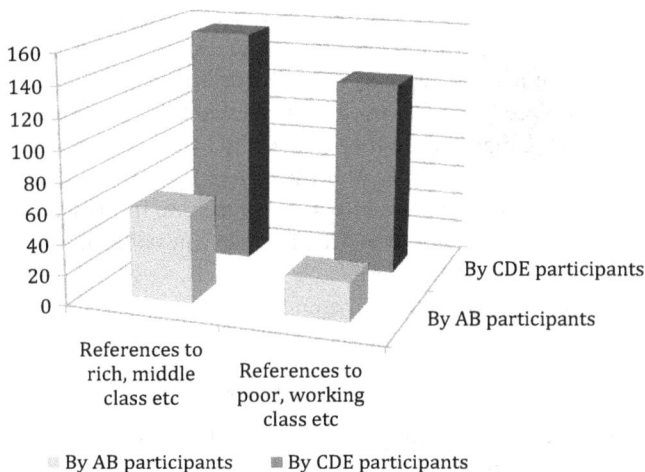

Figure 6.1 Comparing participants' references, by occupational group, to people when talking about 'the economy'

Of the personalising terms both high- and low-income participants use, 'rich' and 'poor' are more popular than others like 'middle class' or 'working class'. In addition, Figure 6.1 shows that whenever participants mention social groups, they mention the rich, middle class etc. more than the poor, working class. They see the rich as more central than the poor to talk about 'the economy', since it is 'the rich who write the rules'.

In a focus group, the depth of Linda's analysis of different districts of the city shows how wide she believes the gulf between 'rich' and 'poor' is. She describes stumbling on a very wealthy enclave in the middle of a council estate.

Linda: Do you know, the strangest thing happened to me yesterday? I was going to B's house and I got lost and I cut down this little road off the main road off Z [lower-income district of the city] and it's like, it's like I went in through a barrier into a different world. These were the most beautiful houses ... it was mortifying, the grass was all beautiful, and every single car was a '17 or '16 number plate. Most of them had motorhomes. I was just driving up this one little road.

Shelley: Yeah I know the road you mean, it is wonderful.

Linda: And it comes to this circle ... and then the next road's bungalows, millions of little beautiful bungalows. Then I drove back out into reality [laughter]. Yeah but they just look different don't they, they even smell different [laughter] ... It's just, it was sunny and that street [laughs, puts her head in her hands], I swear to you I drove into it and there were people doing their gardens, and I thought 'I've got my heating on because I'm cold and they're in their gardens digging up and everything like'. And I'm like 'why did the sun decide to come here? [Laughter] Why is this little road, this little circle, sat in this shitty place [near the larger council estate]? ... Do these people know they live here? [Laughter] Do they know who lives across the road?'

It was just mind blowing ... And I kept looking back at it thinking that's really strange ... like I'd gone into a time machine in my car and ... this is what life could have been like. This is what you could have had, but you ain't! 'Get back out!' [Laughter]

Shelley: 'Get back to your council estate!'

Economic experts

In order to explore understanding of the term 'the economy' we have to also understand the sources of that understanding, any cues that people follow. Who are the economic 'experts' and how much do participants trust them?

The legacy of the 2008 financial crisis looms large even before participants get to the topic of distrust of experts on the European Union. On the surface, both high- and low-income participants are still angry about the bankers. They often associate 'experts' with the financial and economic experts who either colluded in or failed to prevent the 2008 crisis and also see that crisis as having revealed how hand-in-glove these flawed experts were with the government. However, the nature of distrust varies between the two districts.

Church district: no economic giants

I discussed the high level of Church district distrust of unemployment statistics in Chapter 3. Church district participants talk at length about distrust. As Figure 6.2 shows, an NVivo count reveals 38 per cent of the amount of interview transcripts coded as distrust of banks, statistics or experts come from occupational group A/B participants, who make up 40 per cent of participants, which shows that they are *exercised* by this issue almost as much as those from C1, C2, D and E backgrounds.

What are the parameters and features of their distrust? When I ask 'what do you know and understand about banks and the banking system?', assuming many would believe banks contained financial experts, few are positive. The first theme in banks' fall from grace is corruption or greed.

It is 'systematic' and they all collaborate in it. (Fawad)

[Banks] allowed one part of the banking system to infect the other. (Gareth)

[Banks] are run by human beings who are very fallible, who are greedy. (Jane, in her seventies, echoed by Mary, in her seventies, Richard, in his seventies, Johnny, in his thirties, and Joseph, in his seventies)

■ Percentage of statements expressing distrust of banks, unemployment stats and experts by
  occupational group

38.64%

                                          31.36%

                    10.01%   12.73%

                                                                                    7.26%

Occ gp A/B   Occ gp C1   Occ gp C2   Occ gp D   Occ gp E

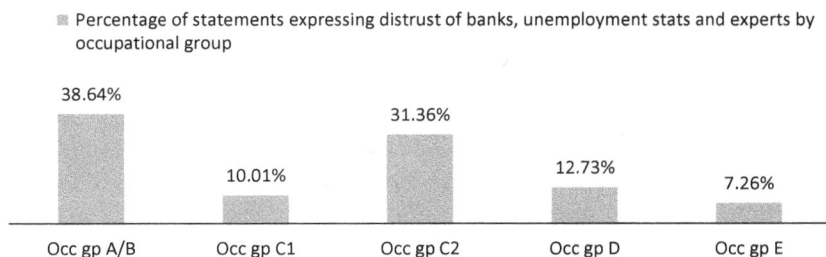

Figure 6.2 Percentage of participants' statements expressing distrust of expertise, by
occupational group

The second related theme is banks' power as huge institutions. There is quite sincere sadness that they have let other institutions and society down. As Jane says:

> You would have thought the banks know what they're talking about but they didn't
> and you still wonder whether they have learned their lesson.

Harry sums up a sense that they could be relied on more in the past, when he talks about his job doing the accounts in the NHS.

> One time we used to say in the health service … 'we wouldn't expect to get this
> amount wrong in the banks so why would you expect it to go wrong in the health
> service?' But it has been slipping for a good twenty years now, so the whole ethos
> and the whole way that banking is done isn't as precise or as safe as I think it was
> at one stage. (Harry)

As well as saddened (Joseph), interviewees were 'horrified' (Jane), thought banks behaved 'abominably' (Rachel) and were 'totally discredited' (Peter) by 2008. Fawad contrasts the lack of bailout for Tata steel with the bank bailouts and Stephanie sums up the tenor of many comments with 'and they don't seem to have suffered from the crash … and the government seems to have bailed them out at everybody else's expense, with no real repercussions', which is 'unfair'.

What do they believe about broader economic expertise such as in academia, the media or government? Some of their beliefs on bankers follow through – Michael says banks have 'excessive power' and 'permeate government'. In focus group one, in answer to an open question, 'Who do you think economic experts are?', participants are stumped for an answer.

Peter: In the country today?
David: I go back to what I said at the beginning that you can get two different
experts with completely opposing views and I find that very, very difficult, I really do. I just don't understand it. As a complete outsider I get the impression that Carney … in the Bank of England is probably a wise man,

although people have hated some things he's said and done. But I haven't got enough knowledge.

James: Carney made some really fundamentally political statements before the referendum about what a disaster it was going to be. It was going to be total collapse immediately and he has now completely changed his tune and says it's an opportunity and so on and so on. So, I don't regard him as a sound economic expert any more. I'm struggling to think.

David: Who is it? Boris? [Laughter]

Jane: These aren't economists. Boris isn't an economist. Isn't it true that people who have won Nobel prizes for economics say different things? You have a recession and you either spend your way out of it or you don't spend your way out of it. I mean common sense it's such a vast, vast topic...

David: It's quite interesting; you asked that question and we are a bit dumbfounded. None of us are saying there's a giant of economics that we would agree this is the person that we wish would sort us out. It isn't there.

Some Church district participants believe we are listening to the wrong experts. Peter continues the thread above by saying:

> And yet we would have done [known who the experts were] in the past; in the '40s and '50s we would unquestionably have said Keynes, in the '70s and '80s people probably would have said Friedman or Hayek.

Elsewhere in his interview, Peter, explicitly backed by a few others such as Michael, attacks the reliance on 'neoliberal' economists, saying their policies have made many people worse off and are in part responsible for the Leave vote in 2016.

> I think where people sort of suddenly sat back and said, 'yeah, it [the economy] is not working, if that's going to be how it is, let's go for it [vote Leave]'. And that was what I think motivated a number of perhaps rather ill-informed and perhaps inexperienced people to vote Leave, they didn't vote Leave from a rational perspective weighing up the pros and cons.

Peter's criticism of neoliberalism is partly pragmatic in that he believes neoliberal economic policies do not deliver sound economy.

> Those assumptions were made and policies were decided on, on the basis they were reasonable. Did it turn out? ... And if it doesn't work then you should replace it, or move it on or do something.

Even among those not explicitly criticising 'neoliberalism', there is criticism of economic expertise and economics as a discipline. James, one of the most favourably disposed towards economics as a discipline, acknowledges that there are 'very complicated macroeconomics' involved in trying to run a country, but in part because of the interaction between economics and politics, 'let's not try and pretend that we can solve all the problems using economics because we often get it wrong'. Many perceive economics as a 'pseudo-science' rather than a pure science like medicine (David). They suspect economists' attempts to present themselves as 'scientists' commenting on an objective reality.

Economists are in reality divided and this reduces how much people can depend on them. Church district participants' comments on the nature of economics, which affect perceptions of economic expertise, include:

> Economics is very subjective; it's not an objective science. You know you have monetarists and you have Keynesians, it's a matter of opinion largely. (Milo,[13] in his twenties)

> And anyway, yeah experts and experts, that's what I mean by two people looking at the same problem, lot of experience and they take diametrically opposing views, and they get quite nasty in their condemnation of the other side as well. (Richard, in his eighties)

> It depends who they are doesn't it? One person says one thing and another person says another. (Alice, in her eighties)

> What confuses me is that you can hear economists who presumably are knowledgeable having completely different opinions and that clearly is confusing for a layperson. (Jane, in her seventies)

> You know, if you said to doctors, 'how do you treat pneumonia?', you wouldn't have great camps of people. They all know. But when it comes to the economy, you get the traditionalists and you've got all these words like Keynesian. (David, in his seventies)

Therefore, many Church district participants believe economic experts are divided; this has taken place against a backdrop of distrust of bankers and statistics such as those on unemployment, compounded by strong criticisms of use of statistics by both sides in the EU campaign.

The focus group leave the subject of economic expertise hanging in the air.

James: On experts, not sure. In the hard sciences in general people, including the press, would say they trust experts. If you want to build a bridge you'd probably best go to a bridge builder, somebody who knows something about bridges. That's not true of economy.

Peter: [Ironic tone] If you want to build an economy you go to an economist?

Hill district: 'experts for the rich'

In Hill district, distrust of 'experts' runs deeper. They also distrusted unemployment statistics and in Chapter 4 I revealed how much they distrusted politicians and those who promoted austerity.

---

[13] Milo does not live in Church district but a similar area.

Some make the general 'experts are divided' point made in Church district. For instance, when I ask 'who do you think are economic experts?' in the Hill district focus group they laugh.

> **Misha:** But again I think it's one of those things that goes down to each individual. What I could view as being good for the economy, Martha could have a completely different opinion about what's better for the economy and Shelley could have a different opinion to that. Who can say they are an expert? An expert for what? For all, for who?

However, from this point in the focus group they continue in a way that diverges from those in Church district.

> **Martha:** An expert for what system do you want?
> **Shelley:** Experts for the rich.

In the exchange above and those following, participants make the same point as the Church district focus group about the divergent ideas of economic experts, but there is an extra dimension. The division is not just as it was in Church district, between beliefs such as Keynesian and monetarist, or, as Martha later adds, the underlying 'standards' experts are basing beliefs on. In Hill district the extra dimension is that experts are seen as representing the already powerful or wealthy. As Misha asks, *who* are they representing: 'an expert for what? For all, for who?' In another exchange she asks:

> **Misha:** Who benefits from it [expertise]?
> **Linda:** Only them.

When I ask whether the governor of the Bank of England is an expert, Shelley answers, 'for him and his lovely money in his bank'. When I ask another low-income focus group what they would say to economists who argue that migration is good for 'the economy', they agree with Beverley that experts are backing employers' profiteering and casualisation of contracts.

> **Beverley:** [The economists] say [migration is] good, because [the employers] don't have to pay so much.

Some do not trust experts because they see them as self-interested.

> No. They talk as if they're only in there for themselves. (Jean)

The self-interested expert 'spinning' is also a more dominant theme than it was in Church district.

> Well the thing is I think people have got ways of getting information. They can put a spin on it, which sometimes makes it sound alright when it actually isn't, or

perhaps things are going the wrong way and you don't know just how bad the thing is because they put a spin on it. So basically I don't necessarily trust the motives of the people that are delivering the information. (Julie)

They think they are [experts]. See they're people who… they must be brainy, mustn't they, to be able to flannel some people. (Steven)

Many participants believe trust has declined over a long period accelerated by 2008. Gary comments on how much distrust of banking has increased, which echoes much of what Church district participants said.

Well basically they spend people's money they haven't got and then the people have to put money back in when banks are back to normal, so it cost people twice. I think they're getting more trustworthy because they're having to be open about things, but I still don't think they tell you everything that's going on. That trust is going to take a long, long time to get back.

There is also a lot of anger among Leave voters in particular about the role of experts in 'Project Fear' during the referendum campaign.

Well they keep getting it wrong, as simple as that. So, if you keep getting it wrong, it's not working. If somebody said this is going to happen, we're going to struggle, we're going to suffer, and the pound's going to be destroyed and that doesn't happen. The same as, anything to do with the future they predict doesn't seem to be true. They seem to be getting it wrong more often than they get it right. Surely you should just say, 'this is what's happening now, in the future it will either go up or down'. Nobody can judge that I don't think [laughs]. But they're smarter than me, so what do I know. (Gary)

Well only that somebody's probably going to tell me a lot of lies or spin me a yarn because they're bluffing and like the Brexit thing. (Julie)

However, there is acknowledgement that the Leave campaign also massaged statistics, as in the £350-million claim,[14] which even UKIP sympathiser George criticises. From outside the focus group, Beverley articulates a distrust of the way *all* politicians used economic statistics in the referendum campaign.

Yeah well I think, okay, he can give me all these figures and everything, but I don't believe them. I don't believe them because I never do believe the figures. To me they sort of pick a number out of the air and they think 'that's a good figure!' It's like when UKIP, they were there and he wanted to say those twenty million this and twenty million that, but when it came to it, he just plucked the number out of the air because nothing was down on paper. And another bloke,

---

[14] Some Leave campaigners claimed leaving the EU would make the UK £350 million a week better off.

the Conservative or Liberal, they pick a number, but when you read it there's nothing written down like that. They do it to scare people. You can tell I'm an old-fashioned person.

It is not clear whether it is her distrust or antipathy to statistics that makes her, as she says, 'an old-fashioned person'. During the referendum campaign, Beverley says she made a big effort to watch the debates and listen to the politicians' arguments, some of which obviously drew on 'economic experts'. But she concludes:

> And after listening to them for several hours, I thought, they haven't said anything, they never said anything that would convince me to either stay or go. I just have to make my own mind up what I think. Them saying this and this and this, they were both contradicting each other, they weren't sort of saying things that I would have thought 'oh, you're telling the truth there!' Well I didn't think they were telling the truth anywhere so, when I hear things like that I think pah! [Sighs.]

Essentially therefore, the nature of distrust in Hill district is deeper. They distrust experts as a group as part of the rigged economy. In Church district there is distrust because of past performance and division within economics, but not as much. For instance, Church district participants follow economic news more. There is greater hope that experts may redeem themselves.

Conclusion

It is difficult to interview people about their understanding of 'the economy', which may be one reason why so few political writers have attempted it. As one of the focus group participants says, he can talk about aspects like taxation but 'it becomes more imprecise when you're using a general word like economy because it could mean different things and people could interpret it [differently]'. This chapter shows that there are many different interpretations, understandings or representations of 'the economy' in people's minds. However, the answers to questions I outline in this chapter build on my findings in other chapters to elaborate on what people understand by 'the economy' and the understandings that emerge from each district are strikingly different.

In Church district, 'the economy' is an umbrella term for interconnected forces yet it is closer to their everyday lives. They use the term more. They have varying degrees of interest and understanding of its technicalities, but they all recognise it as a phenomenon that they contribute to and that broadly speaking benefits them. They are, to a surprising degree, critical of the turn 'the economy' has taken in recent years, which many believe shows it is not working as it once did. In Polanyian terms, they are uneasy at the degree of its disembeddedness from society.

In Hill district, there are a few, mainly older, participants who do not conceptualise 'the economy' as an umbrella term for economic activity. Many others in Hill district do perceive it as an umbrella term but feel less connected to it. There is more of a gulf between their everyday economic lives of working and living and 'the economy' compared with Church district. They are more critical of 'the economy', which many see as benefiting the rich. Their distrust of expertise is deeper.

Formal and rigged versions of 'the economy' in Brexit Britain

Field diary entry three months after the 2016 referendum, in a politics seminar

The afternoon is cloudy but stuffy and we are in one of the high-rise blocks consisting of lecture and seminar rooms. There would be a good view of the city but from this angle I can only see the sky. Political scientists are discussing why Leave won. They are arguing about what role economic factors played either through people's socioeconomic status as 'left behind' or their beliefs. There is a consensus that many Leave voters opposed migration. Someone says this reflects long-held values of fear of the 'Other' and socio-cultural resistance to change. The survey evidence shows that. Someone speculates whether that opposition to migration might have been in part economic. He says 'maybe Leave voters believed migration would damage the economy?' Another political scientist responds, 'they might have done, but they were wrong'. [Laughter.]

In Brexit Britain, how do people understand the term 'the economy?' In this concluding chapter I draw together the evidence from the fieldwork. I first describe the two dominant understandings that emerged: an understanding of 'the economy' as to some extent formal, but with reservations, from high-income Church district, and an understanding of it as rigged from low-income Hill district. In the second section I attempt explanations for them. I argue that participants see 'the economy' through the lenses of their own experience, and that the experiences that are most important are economic, such as income levels, rather than those relating to gender or age. I argue that income shapes underlying understandings of 'the economy' even when people have different political beliefs and go on to vote for different political parties or economic policies. I consider the role of education, which some will argue is more significant than income. I turn to a theme that is an undercurrent throughout this book: trust in expertise. Trust in economic expertise seems to be a circular phenomenon. How people understand the term 'the economy' may affect how predisposed they are to trust economic experts, and at the same time perceptions of economic expertise may shape understandings of the term 'the economy'. I draw on survey evidence on trust and explore whether there may be economic or sociological reasons for distrust as well as those often categorised as 'cultural'.

Church district's formal version

I argued in Chapter 1 that many political scientists and mainstream politicians understand 'the economy' to be a neutral term for impersonal forces in some way distinct from more human spheres such as the social or cultural, a 'formal' understanding based on neoclassical economics. This book suggests that Church district participants share that understanding more than Hill district ones do.

Church district participants see 'the economy' as an *umbrella*, both in the sense that their everyday life is connected to it and in the sense that the economic forces under it are connected with each other. Chapter 6 shows Church district participants may express some feelings of disconnection from the recently more disembedded economy of the neoliberal decades, but their belief that, generally, they are more connected is reflected in the fact that they are three times more likely to use the term 'the economy' in their interviews than low-income participants. They are more positive about 'the economy' than those in Hill district, which implies a greater degree of connection; they see it as 'the ship of state' and are 'cheerleaders' who 'want to see success'. As well as the term 'economy', they use prefixes like 'our' and 'British' in the normal course of the interviews. They are more prepared to describe their referendum vote as 'economic', seeing no stigma in it. Church district participants believe they *contribute* to 'the economy'.

Church district participants also acknowledge interconnection between the forces under 'the economy' umbrella, which they see as encompassing more. On employment, Church district participants show how 'inter-connected' the official economic forces are in the way they talk about low pay as damaging, even though they personally are not experiencing it. They are more likely to talk of the effects of technological change, the decline in manufacturing and global competition as part of the general impact of 'the economy' on employment. They give examples of how inflation might cause interest rate rises, or the referendum the fall in the value of sterling. They recognise government attempts to steer 'the economy', such as in the drive to reduce the deficit.

Church district participants also to a large degree see 'the economy' as impersonal forces in the sense that there are laws, such as of supply and demand, and increasingly global movements of capital and products, presented as beyond human control. Their unease at the extent of disembeddedness in recent years is not significant enough to amount to the focus on economic relations that I explore in the rigged version below. They speak of the 'playing field becoming less level' in recent times, but are saddened by that process because of how *excessive* it has been; some tweaking will soon make the playing field level enough again. To Church district participants, there is a definite article in their talk on 'the economy' and a sense of it as rightly separate from the 'human element'. Some of them talk about it as a more technical sphere, a sphere where there should be a more genuinely 'scientific' approach, a sphere about which experts should be less divided.

Hill district's rigged version

One example of the greater disconnect from 'the economy' expressed by Hill district participants relates to government debt (Chapter 4). Hill district participants' understanding of personal debt affects their beliefs about government debt; they are so concerned about personal debt that they see it as more important than government debt, which makes them less receptive to the household debt analogy than those in Church district. It could be argued that conducting these interviews after 2016, when government debt is a less salient issue than before, replaced by Brexit, accounts for some of this lack of awareness of the seriousness of government debt in Hill district, but Church district participants *are* still aware of it.

This Hill district narrative of disconnection reflects the pattern emerging from their everyday economies, that they have a *deep but narrower* interaction with the 'official' economy (Chapter 6). 'The economy' is a less *all-encompassing* umbrella. Hill district participants do not tend to have shares, mortgages or savings and may only have access to payday loans rather than those based on compound interest. They interact with the 'official' economy intensely, such as through employment, but at fewer points.

The fieldwork suggests lower-income participants understand 'the economy' to be less impersonal, and arguably therefore less distinct from human spheres, in that they believe the rich play a bigger part in controlling the forces than higher-income participants do. In Chapter 6 I show that low-income participants make three times more references to *people* in their interviews and focus groups than high-income ones, particularly 'the rich', with 'the poor' in second place for frequency. I argue in Chapter 6 that a term that encapsulates this theme is that the economy is 'rigged'. What do the participants in this study mean by 'rigged'? I showed how Hill district participants often understand 'the economy' to be rigged because the rich write the rules. Rosa, in her forties, is articulate on this subject. 'The economy' 'rips people off' and represents itself falsely; it is a 'ruse' because in fact the real work is done by 'grafters' on low incomes who do not see the benefits.

In Chapter 3, 'rigged' comes out in Hill district beliefs that they work hard but wages stay low, employment statistics mask the truth. In Chapter 4, 'rigged' is reflected in the 'lie' that we would all be in austerity together. In Hill district, even if there are some differing levels of criticism of the 'workshy' on benefits, they are united in their perception of austerity as having hit low-income people disproportionately hard, through cuts in benefits, social housing or overstretched welfare and health services. In Chapter 5, 'rigged' is reflected in the belief that people on low incomes suffer more from the costs of migration in terms of pressure on unskilled wages, growth of zero-hours contracts and reduced welfare services, while not receiving as much economic benefit from it as higher-income groups. Successive governments' support for free movement has rigged the system against them. In contrast, many Church district participants have a positive everyday understanding of the economic effects of migration because they have worked abroad or do not experience the same pressure on housing or welfare. Migration is beneficial to them as employers who welcome 'lively, educated people'. Differing everyday economic circumstances appear to affect how much participants fear the localised effects of economic challenges posed by openness and the increased supply of labour.

Hill district participants feel more dissociated from the official version of 'the economy' of mainstream politicians and the media. Chapters 5 and 6 show they are not only reluctant to use the term 'economy', but when they do use the term it is not prefaced by 'our' or 'British' and is often negative. They are sometimes reluctant to describe their own political behaviour in the referendum as 'economic' (Chapter 5) even when they have described reasons for voting, whether for Remain or Leave, that link with concerns about jobs or industry.

Other recent ethnographic research (New Economic Foundation 2018) finds that many of their respondents believe the reason 'the economy' is like it is because 'the economic system is rigged'. NEF cites survey evidence from Populus (2016) that 74 per cent believe the UK's economic system effective in providing opportunities for people from wealthy backgrounds, but only 5 per cent believe it is effective for people from poor backgrounds. NEF are searching for 'shared' cultural models and do not break their 'rigged' findings down according to income, but this study indicates perceptions of 'rigged' are more extensive and deep-rooted among those from low incomes.

In Chapter 1 I outlined a critical strand in political economy that understands each historically contingent 'economy' as situated in broader structures of 'economic relations', social and political structures and power relationships. I also outlined Polanyian thought about how market societies reframe provisioning for life as a formal 'economy' that is disembedded from social relationships. 'Rigged' from Hill district does seem to resonate with Polanyian thought in that 'the economy' is perceived as distinct from society. However, the overwhelming emphasis on the rich writing the rules makes it, on balance, closer to the critical 'economic relations' version.

Why do understandings vary?

I approached the research with an open mind about what patterns in understanding might emerge. I chose to research in two contrasting districts, low-income Hill district and high-income Church district, as a device to ensure I could reach people from a range of incomes, not because I assumed the main patterns that would emerge would reflect income. In fact my hunches before I started were that political beliefs, gender and age might affect people's understanding as much as their income level. However, each time I analysed the transcripts, whether on themes like employment, austerity or trade and migration, the pattern that was most striking was between the districts. There were a few high-income people living in Hill district. They seemed more aware of problems of personal debt or poverty from neighbours' experiences, but they did not share their neighbours underlying understandings of 'the economy'. My argument is that personal experiences of 'the economy' shape understanding of the term 'the economy'. In this section I set out that case and then consider whether and how political beliefs, gender, age or education seem to affect understandings.

Seeing 'the economy' through the lens of experience of it

This study supports the conclusions of other ethnographers, such as Lane (1962), Gamson (1992) and Cramer (2016); personal experience acts as a lens through which people observe the wider world. The question is *which* experiences are most important. In the case of viewing 'the economy', I argue their experiences of it seem to act as the main element to the lens.

When I ask participants to recount their economic life histories, they are emotional and sometimes even raw, with memories of hunger and of being made redundant several times. Present-day economic experiences are also powerful, in some cases all-encompassing and overwhelming. Participants often answer my questions about the more general concepts of 'employment' or 'trade' by using personal examples. While it could be argued that starting an interview with an invitation to 'tell your economic life story' makes it likely interviews will contain talk about both the personal and the abstract economy, even the couple of participants who are reluctant to tell a life story bring personal experience into their later answers on employment and trade.

I illustrate how all participants draw on personal experiences of 'the economy' with Jean and Peter. Jean is in her seventies. She tells me her personal economic experiences are that she has budgeted closely, never getting into debt, and 'got through' a lifetime of hard manual work for secure but low wages. Jean and her husband rent a one-bedroom flat, do not go on holidays and can only just afford to run a car. They live on state pensions. She does not follow the economic news because she says:

> We know we're going to get no more money than what they give us, the state give us, so what's the use of it you know? They say 'oh yes we'll give you £7 extra a week'.

Well where does that £7 go? The rent and the community charge, it's gone – that's how it goes, believe me.

As I show in Chapter 6, when I ask her whether she understands the 'national economy', she answers: 'I don't know a lot about *the* economy really'. Nevertheless, while Jean may not follow '*the* economy' closely, she distinguishes it from her personal economy, even if just in the form of policy on pension rises affecting her provisioning. Her personal experiences of physical hard work, only ever just 'getting through' and struggling on the pension, affect how she sees 'the economy' and her desire to distance herself from it, since she has no power and does not want to dwell on her position as being so dependent on those annual pension decisions. Peter, with a higher income but also in his seventies, follows '*the* economy' more closely; he devours economic news and books from Hayek to Piketty. However, he also brings in his personal experiences often in his talk about it. His personal economic experiences are that he was 'lucky' enough to go from grammar school to university, from university to secure employment at a senior executive level, with an appreciating asset in the shape of a house. In his answers on employment, while he brings in his wider reading, he still focuses on his personal experiences at the top of a company at the forefront of automation. When I ask about migration, he responds with official statistics, but also mentions beliefs of family members and how it impacted on his own job opportunities. This finding echoes the conclusions of Cramer and Toff (2017), who find elected officials and 'experts' draw on their personal experiences as much as the 'less expert'. Despite the differences in their economic circumstances and the degree of interest they profess to take in 'the economy', Jean and Peter both to some extent see 'the economy' through the lenses of their personal economic experiences.

What are those personal economic experiences, as recounted in the previous chapters? Chapter 3 shows that in Hill district the common experience of low pay and a shortage of affordable housing means most understand their everyday economies to be a 'struggle'. In contrast, in Church district, rising wages and appreciating house prices mean participants understand their everyday circumstances to be 'comfortable' and 'secure'. Church district participants' main everyday economic concerns are about their children. In Church district, everyday understanding of employment is different from that in Hill district; the majority of participants over forty have experienced more stable careers and control over them as well as higher salaries than those in Hill district. In contrast, in Hill district, participants have less control over employment.

In Chapter 4, everyday understanding of personal debt varies. Hill district participants fear it, often driven into it to pay essential bills due to the precarity of employment. For them, personal debt is of the nightmarish payday loan variety since many more reputable lenders will not give them credit. If they are not in debt themselves they know others who are, and they are particularly fearful about young people getting into debt. Hill district's participants' fear of personal debt means some of the moral condemnation of it they may have inherited from their parents has been worn away. In contrast, in Church district, everyday understanding of personal debt is that it is due to profligacy and materialism and can be avoided with willpower; they have been able to maintain the traditions that taught them to see it as immoral.

Gender

Do participants' gender-related experiences shape understandings of 'the economy'? In Chapter 1 I note that some feminist economists are developing an understanding of 'the economy' that is broad and close to Polanyian concepts of social provisioning that includes unpaid work caring for family members. They argue that women's understandings, in particular of 'the economy', are excluded by formalist or neoclassical approaches. My fieldwork suggests that even in a less expansive research design where the aspects of 'the economy' I ask about are mainstream ones heard on the media that do not include unpaid work, women's understandings are different to men's in two ways.

First, on the *content* of women's understanding of 'the economy', as Chapter 6 shows, women are more likely to refer to the micro level or household in their definitions of 'the economy', indicating support for the feminist position that women see 'the economy' as about provisioning and as more rooted in the everyday.

Second, a lot of the literature on factual knowledge about the mainstream economy and attitudes to financial knowledge shows women to be less confident than men. They see 'the economy' as more of a male-dominated sphere (Ferber et al. 1983; Brückner et al. 2015). This finding is reflected in more female participants in this study saying they feel less confident talking about it than the male participants; only 8 per cent of participants who express 'confidence' in their understanding of 'the economy' are women. However, women's lack of confidence does not accurately reflect the depth and complexity of statements they make in the interviews, another common finding of those who undertake mixed-method studies (O'Connor 2012; Williamson and Wearing 1996). Women such as Jean have often been the chief 'provisioners' making the daily decisions about what food to buy and coping with emotional fallout and impact on family relationships. Women's contributions are among the most animated, complex and sophisticated of all participants (see Rosa on 'the economy' as a 'ruse' or Jane on how it is not a 'black box' in Chapter 6).

However, despite the shared lack of confidence in understanding of 'the economy' and intensity of feeling about the provisioning, there are profound *differences* between the economic experiences of women in Hill and Church district documented throughout this study. Jane from Church district was brought up in a low-income family and is the same age as Jean from Hill district. Both are in their seventies. However, as an adult Jane has always had a well-paid, secure, professional career, owns a large house, has spent time abroad working and on extended holidays, has not had to budget or even follow tax policy closely and her only economic concern is how much she will be able to give to her grand-children. Her understanding of the official economy is close to that of other Church district participants; she trusts experts more, perceives 'the economy' to be impersonal forces and follows it closely. In contrast, Jean has always budgeted on a low wage and has not had holidays abroad. While she 'manages' on the state pension she is more vulnerable to rent increases, utility price rises, changes in council policy on her housing, and her husband not being able to drive anymore because a lack of buses means having to depend on taxis she cannot afford. She worries about the quality of jobs that will be available to her grandchildren and that they might even end up experiencing greater poverty than she did. As we have already seen, Jean shares much with other Hill district participants in not following 'the economy' closely. Therefore I argue that, while gender may shape understanding, economic circumstances exert a more powerful force.

Age

Age shapes understanding of the term 'the economy' in some key respects. Chapter 6 shows it is mainly older participants, from both districts, who express strong socio-cultural opposition to migration (see also Ford and Lymperopoulou 2017). In contrast, the eighteen-year-olds in the sixth-form college, including those from low-income backgrounds, tend not to see migration 'as a problem' on any level, socio-cultural or economic. It is mainly older participants who believe that the UK can benefit significantly from trade with the Commonwealth post-Brexit. Older voters are more likely to perceive the physical overcrowding resulting from migration as problematic, not acknowledging the perspective of younger participants that the capacity of a state's infrastructure to expand is more important than the numbers of migrants.

Age is the key component affecting political behaviour according to Inglehart and Norris's 'post materialism' thesis (2016, 2019). They argue that people's early socialisation is important and that cohorts move through life, for instance, attached to authoritarian values, rather than all cohorts becoming more authori-tarian as they become older. They claim that even after controlling for social backgrounds, the generational gap in authoritarian values remains 'significant and large' (2019:111). However, while there is a lot of survey evidence to back Inglehart and Norris's argument that older people are more authoritarian, there is not survey evidence I can draw on about their underlying views of 'the economy'. On the basis of this study, I am sceptical about whether understanding of 'the economy' varies much according to age. As with gender, there is much common ground between low-income eighteen-year-olds and low-income eighty-year-olds. Even at eighteen, low-income young people who have watched their parents ground down by hard physical work and long hours fear for their own future and fear university debt more than their high-income counterparts. Low-income participants in their twenties and thirties have experienced greater numbers of job changes, less secure employment contracts and arguably lower real wages and higher housing costs than those in their seventies. Nevertheless, those older low-income participants have often experienced hunger in their childhoods and are acutely aware of modern conditions through the experiences of children and grandchildren. Low-income participants, whether young or old, share an understanding of 'the economy' as rigged to some degree.

While high-income young participants are conscious they may have a future with less secure employment and housing than their parents, they are nevertheless more optimistic and dread 'the economy' less than their lower-income counterparts.

Political beliefs

One reason why the talk about 'the economy' in this study is so open and revealing is that I was asking '*what do you understand* about trade, employment and so on' rather than putting participants on the spot by asking them '*what do you believe?*' or '*which policy do you support?*' The latter style of questioning may force people to search for beliefs they do not actually have (Campbell and Converse 1960). Similarly, I kept direct questions about which parties participants usually voted for in general elections or how they voted in the referendum (although referendum votes were often volunteered) towards the end of the interviews.

A sign that economic circumstances shape underlying understanding of 'the economy' is that they seem to do so even when participants support parties with different economic policies. This insight is an important one, overlooked by surveys that ask participants to select which left/right policy options they support without exploring their underlying understanding of 'the economy' itself. *Why* it might happen, why a shared underlying understanding of 'the economy' does not lead people to vote for the same economic policies, is beyond the scope of the book. The book explores what understandings are rather than why certain understandings lead people to vote the way they do.

I illustrate the finding that people share some underlying understanding of 'the economy' according to income and regardless of political belief with Hill district Martin's beliefs. As a Conservative, he is opposed to what he sees as excessive taxation for people on his kind of wage as a supervisor in a security firm. He believes the NHS is 'a bottomless pit' and that Labour is too 'frivolous' about public spending and government debt. However, despite his support for Conservative economic *policies*, he shares much of his understanding of 'the economy' with other more left-wing low-income participants. For instance, he believes his own everyday economy has not been rewarded for the effort he puts in.

It's always been about hard work. It's go out and earn your money, but then it's whether you've got the money to spend at the end of it.

He distrusts economic experts and politicians, arguing that 'the economy' is 'extremely manipulated, by politicians'. He expresses anger at how rigged the system has been post-2008, saying:

There's a great saying in a recession: the rich get richer, which definitely happens. You see it all the time, people are scrimping and saving, scraping to buy anything and you've got people buying supercars, paintings worth millions of pounds because they see it as an investment ... It's an upside-down pyramid in wealth. The top 1 per cent have got pretty much the whole wealth, certainly if you look across the world the top 5 per cent own 90 per cent of the wealth. How can that be justified?

He also has a localised perspective, suspecting that London drives 'the economy'.

Similarly, one of Hill district's other Conservatives, Beverley, shows her support for a Conservative perspective on social class by arguing that anyone, including the rich, should be counted as working class. She supports low-tax policies and tough benefit policies consistent with her Conservative affiliation, yet she still shares with other Hill district participants deep distrust of political and economic elites and makes statements like 'I never do believe the figures' and 'I don't like listening to the news at all because I think, oh no, it's so depressing, it depresses me' (Chapter 6).

In the same way, left-wing Church district participant Peter still shares an underlying understanding of 'the economy' as largely impersonal forces with more right-wing Church district participants (Chapter 6). Political affiliation makes a difference in the case of the Keynesian ten (Chapter 4), as all those who express support for Keynesian *policies* regarding national debt are left of centre, but as far as underlying understanding of 'the economy' is concerned, political affiliation does not seem to make as much difference as economic circumstances.

Education

Some political scientists argue that education affects understanding rather than experiences of 'the economy' or income levels. The reason that high-income participants understand 'the economy' as formal is because they have spent more years in education and have the sophistication to generalise and the ability to understand the economic news. In essence, as the neoclassical economists

I mentioned in Chapter 1 argue, it is not a different understanding that low-income people have – it is a *lack* of understanding.

Some commentators argue education is becoming more important than economic circumstances in explaining why people vote the way they do (Kaufmann 2017). For Inglehart and Norris, education is significant, in part because it affects socialisation. Since World War II, increasing proportions of young people have gone to university. They argue that receiving a university-level education makes people more liberal; 'education is consistently associated with attitudes that are more tolerant toward out-groups, including ethnic, religious and racial minorities' (2019:111). The correlation between education and liberal beliefs persists even with controls for income levels (2019:112).

However, Inglehart and Norris, like many other scholars, recognise that *how* education might be affecting beliefs is complex (2019:112). Some argue it might affect cultural beliefs because it is a 'liberalising' experience (in a UK context, see Surridge 2016), some that it affects beliefs because it makes people more confident they will be able to exploit the economic opportunities offered by globalisation. For instance, Park and Kim (2018) argue that the importance of skill levels has been overlooked in recent analyses of why people voted Leave. Others argue education either reflects cognitive ability because people with higher cognitive ability stay in education for longer, or improves cognitive ability because it makes people more able to generalise and reason in sophisticated ways. Many economists, for instance, believe that education, particularly if it includes some economics, makes people more receptive to economists' arguments, often more complex than common sense or 'folkloric' or naïve' understandings of 'the economy' (Walstad and Larsen 1992; Walstad and Rebeck 2002; Caplan 2002, 2008).

Most of the high-income participants in this study are university-educated and most of the low-income participants are not, with many of those over 40 having left school by 16. Therefore it is difficult to disentangle the effect of education from economic experiences or income in this study. However, as I noted in Chapter 6, it was quite striking that sometimes participants with university education would tell me they followed the 'economic news' closely. If they had a particularly strong interest in politics or economics, they then also often talked in some depth about it, but this was equally true of low-income participants who had not received university-level education. Some of those higher-income participants who had degrees in subjects unrelated to 'the economy' or politics showed sketchy understanding, including not even being aware of government debt. What was striking was not that they seemed to have greater cognitive ability or sophistication, but that they had a wider *range* of direct experiences which might have helped them answer often skewed factual knowledge tests, a subject I explore further in Killick (2017a, 2017b) and a greater willingness to trust in economic expertise, a desire to follow elite cues.

I noted in Chapter 5 that there was much talk by some Church district participants of 'other, less educated' people voting to leave the European Union solely because they were culturally opposed to migration and misinformed about it. In the Church district focus group, when I said my preliminary findings were about how different understandings of 'the economy' were, they assumed I meant in the sense of low-income understanding being *less* in some way, and were concerned in case such statements they had made in interviews about 'other, less educated people' would be seen as elitist. In contrast, in the two lower-income participants' focus groups there was a more immediate understanding of what I was trying to say. Linda commented about higher-income participants that they do not know *more* – instead, 'they know what's interesting to them'.

The difference in understanding I describe in this study does not reflect *lack* of understanding or sophistication about 'the economy' among those with fewer years in education; some of the most perceptive talk was from those in the low-income district who had left school at sixteen.

Trust in expertise

The charge of lack of knowledge, of not being in touch or understanding the full impact of 'the economy' or localised conditions, was levelled by some participants at 'experts'.

Church district participants, as I show in Chapter 6, are more interested in the economic news and more trusting of 'economic experts'. They are critical of economists, but mainly because they are divided, not on the neoclassical fundamentals, but on the policy prescriptions, such as whether to go in a more neo-Keynesian direction. Their distrust is of how experts, including financial experts, and those in banking have *behaved* in recent years, rather than expertise itself.

There is survey evidence that indicates trust in expertise is declining (Edelman Trust 2017), some of which links the decline to the 2008 crash and deteriorating economic conditions (Torcal 2014; Wroe 2014, 2015; Kroknes et al. 2015). There is considerable survey evidence that distrust is higher among low-income compared with high-income people (Alesina and Ferrera 2002; Li et al. 2005; Leiser et al. 2010; Bennett and Kottasz 2012; Edelman Trust 2017).

I argue in Chapter 6 that Hill district participants' distrust of expertise is more deep-rooted than in Church district and should also be interpreted as part of 'rigged', since they perceive experts as helping 'the rich to write the rules'. Various explanations have been put forward for what most agree is a rising level of distrust in expertise in recent years particularly among those on lower incomes. Which of these explanations for rising levels of distrust among lower-income people does this study support the most?

Runciman is one scholar who emphasises how experts may have become more associated with 'the rich' due to sociological reasons (2016, 2017). He argues the expansion in higher education has meant that the entire UK elite, whether politician, civil servant or businessperson, now tend to be university-educated. Graduates are also more socially stratified than before, existing in their own bubble to the extent that he calls them a tribe. Whereas in the past low-income people might have perceived elite status and vested interest as related to income and wealth, now they *also* see it as related to education. Therefore, they are less likely to perceive an expert, inevitably highly educated, as an independent or neutral boffin-like figure who can be trusted, and more likely to associate him or her with the rest of the elite. Runciman argues the fact that 'almost all the winners are educated … gives the impression that knowledge has become a proxy for influence', speaking 'for the worldview of the people who possess it'. It puts the privileged in an even stronger position than in the past, because when they are promoting their own worldview they can dress it up as 'expertise', which 'stinks of hypocrisy' to the less educated (2016).

These participants support the Runciman thesis that there is anger at the hypocrisy and close relationship between rich elites and experts, but his argument that the roots of the anger lie in a general identification of the educated as elites is less supported. Participants only make a couple of references to intelligence or education when they discuss experts, such as Steven and Gary (Chapter 6). Instead, low-income participants' anger is usually couched in terms of the experts' *record* of backing elite interests in recent years. Watson (2017) provides insights here about distrust of experts' records in his analysis of the 2016 referendum result when he elaborates on why many lower-income participants did not trust the Osborne message to vote Remain 'for the sake of the economy', which I outlined in Chapter 1. Like Runciman, Watson argues the distrust has been building for a long time, which this study's finding in Chapter 3, of distrust of employment statistics going back to the 1980s, reflects. Any initial distrust seems to have been deepened by the 2008 crisis: banks' betrayal of trust in the and the governments' failure to 'punish' them. Watson claims that Osborne betrayed trust further when he broke his 2010 promise that everyone would be in austerity together, again supported by these findings (Chapter 4). Therefore, when it came to the referendum campaign, low-income voters could not trust messages like Osborne's Treasury forecast that every household would lose £4,300 from a Leave victory. Watson argues when a household's income is only a few thousand above £4,300, such claims are less credible than when a household's income is high enough that £4,300 really could mean the difference between holidays or a new conservatory. Watson says focus groups in the campaign showed Osborne's £4,300 claim in particular was so *in*credible that the Remain campaign dropped it and dropped Osborne himself in the later stages. Referencing sources like the 2016 Joseph Rowntree Trust report (Wright and Case 2016) he argues low-income

Leave voters, having experienced decades of relative deprivation, stagnating real wages and austerity, had little trust that their future economic prospects would improve.

> These are people for whom rejoicing at the news that 'the economy' is successful seems to be an invitation to marvel at other people's lives, and for whom rescuing 'the economy' appears to involve talk of sacrifices that all-too-quickly land at their door. (Watson 2017:18–9)

The distrust is so deep that Watson's conclusion is that:

> The referendum result can be explained inter alia as a rejection of the political abstraction of 'the economy' as it had come to be used in the UK. (2017:19)

Most economic experts are not engaging in debate with low-income participants. The key battleground of the economic effects of migration proves they do not always provide answers to the questions lower-income participants are asking. The everyday observation of the localised supply-and-demand effects of migration for many low-income participants, including those with no socio-cultural racism or xenophobia, leads them to reason that migration undercuts wages. What answers do economic experts have for them? They have conducted many studies which show that, at the aggregate level, migration boosts GDP and that it either does not undercut wages or boosts them *overall* (Dhingra et al. 2016; Jaumotte et al. 2016; OECD 2014). However, one study that models the effects of migration on different occupational sectors reveals that unskilled and semi-skilled workers may suffer lower pay as a result of migration more than skilled sector workers (Nickell and Saleheen 2015). Nickell and Saleheen find that immigrants in recent years are 'most predominant' in low-skill occupations, the rise has been greatest in those occupations and that, in the semi/unskilled service sector, for example, a 10 per cent rise in the proportion of immigrants is associated with a 2 per cent reduction in pay. They note 'these findings accord well with intuition and anecdotal evidence, but do not seem to have been recorded previously in the empirical literature'. Such analyses of the impact of wages on sectors are not prominent in the media, or when they are mentioned are presented as minor problems. Economic commentator Rolphe (2016), for instance, states in a blog just before the referendum, 'we know that any statistical effects of migration on jobs and wages are very small'.

Many low-income participants in this study, conscious that their city's population has expanded in recent years due to migration from the rest of the EU, also believe continued free movement will lead to more zero-hours contracts. What studies have experts done on whether they are right in their 'localised' reasoning? Economists have been slow to conduct research on the effect of migration on job insecurity or growth in zero-hours contracts, because they say it would be impossible to model (Doherty 2016). More recently, Clark et al. (2017) find migration from new EU member states has boosted the proportion of construction workers who are self-employed and also 'contributed to the trend towards the growing use of zero-hours contracts', even if in a 'limited' way.

A lack of localised research, reflecting local knowledge of conditions on the ground on the subjects people feel affect them, fuels the perception that experts are out of touch and 'don't live like we do' and contributes to the reasons why low-income participants either do not seek out their research, or reject it (Chapters 4, 5 and 6). It perhaps makes people less likely to attempt to see a bigger picture of how much migration contributes to the economy overall.

Conclusion

In conclusion, the fieldwork suggests that income and people's experiences of 'the economy' exert a significant influence on their understandings of the term 'the economy'. The understanding that emerges from high-income Church district is similar to that dominant in the formal version of the economy, while that emerging from low-income Hill district is closer to a version of the economy as 'economic relations' where the forces of the economy are not seen as so distinct from human life, because those who have money write the rules and rig the system to exaggerate its impersonal and 'beyond control' features. In the final chapter, I explore some of the implications of these findings.

'Economically, something new, something different'

Field diary entry, Autumn 2016

Gary is in his forties and was brought up in poverty: 'money was tight'. He has worked in a range of jobs including the army, foundries and retail and now feels settled in the health sector. He is the only wage earner for his partner and their two children and is working many extra hours on a training course to get promotion 'for their futures'. He does not oppose immigration. He thinks a lot of Leave voters were 'hitting back' at the government. He says '50 per cent' of his reasons for voting Leave were economic. He wants 'economically, something new, something different, something not thought about'.

In this chapter I explore the implications of the fieldwork for how we as political scientists should interrogate our own understandings and assumptions when categorising the understandings of others. Do political scientists categorise what 'the economy' and 'economic' are in the same way as ordinary people? In what ways do the economic and non-economic strands of people's beliefs entwine? Is how people understand 'the economy' changing and how should that affect judgements about the importance people attach to 'the economy' when acting politically?

Where does 'the economy' begin and end?

Some political scientists rightly argue we need to be careful about any simplistic presentations of explanations as *either* cultural *or* economic. For instance, Hopkin argues that 'economics and identity are often presented as opposing hypotheses' but that 'this analytical distinction is misleading' (2017b:475). Mitchell (2008b) argues that because the concept of 'the economy' developed at the same time as social sciences, and therefore strong demarcation lines were drawn by disciplines such as sociology and economics as they attempted to establish their identities, this helps to explain why we have arrived at a situation where 'to conventional ways of thinking, economy and culture stand as opposites' (2008b:447), with 'the economy' seen as the sphere of material needs and culture as the sphere of values.

I argued in Chapter 1 that the neoclassical conception of 'the economy' as *particularly* distinct from the human and the cultural – assuming rationality and self-interested behaviour, governed by laws that operate beneath the surface – appears to exert a powerful influence within the discipline of political science. As political scientists we should be open to the possibility that we have been trained to categorise 'economy' or 'economic' in a certain way, but others may not categorise it in the same way.

I accept that because the first response many participants in this study give to the question 'how would you define the economy?' is that it is 'to do with money', that at some level most people understand 'the economy' to be about the material realm, money or what money can buy. In contrast, the cultural, whether the emotional, moral or social, is about the non-material. However, the more controversial aspect of categorisation is what else people bring in to that description of 'the economy' as 'to do with money', the other baggage the term brings with it. The baggage high-income participants bring in to their understanding of 'the economy' may be less obvious to political scientists. High-income people approach survey questions on 'the economy' confident they know what the person asking the questions means by the term. They see 'the economy' as more connected to their own economies and as a phenomenon at least with the potential to benefit, so that they can apply their everyday reasoning to the question with ease. However, lower-income people may hesitate about whether to answer the political scientists' survey questions with their own perspective or to give an answer which correlates with what they know is the 'official' line on the national economy in the media. Our lack of curiosity about the pictures that go through people's minds when they see the term 'the economy' in survey questions means we may miss the possibility, suggested by this study, that the baggage low-income people bring in means they approach survey questions with the word 'economy' in them with a greater feeling of dissonance than high-income people. This greater sense of negativity and dissonance may be one reason why low-income participants in this study are less prepared to use the term 'the economy' or label their own votes as 'economic' even when they express material reasons for them. The sense that there *could* be a different version of 'the economy' they could one day relate to is reflected in talk by some in Chapter 6 of 'the economy' as needing to be about 'stability' and 'value', Gary's search for 'economically something … not thought about' or Misha's desire that 'the economy' should be about 'the savings but also civility'.

Sometimes there seems to be a lack of consistency in the application of the labels 'economic' or 'cultural' to beliefs. Political scientists who believe cultural drivers are becoming most important in political behaviour, challenging the previous orthodoxy that 'the economy' was, have sometimes categorised what are beliefs about the material world as cultural. This has been clearest in the case of migration. Survey evidence from the regular 'does immigration damage the economy?' and 'does immigration undermine culture?' questions asked by British

Social Attitudes and British Election Studies suggest there is an economic component to opposition to migration because people opposed to migration usually answer yes to both questions (Ford and Lymperopoulou 2017). Although there has been a decline in high-income respondents believing migration damages 'the economy' in recent years, there has been no comparable shift in low-income respondents' beliefs, suggesting low-income people do still believe there is an economic component that relates to issues like wages and competition for resources. This study also suggests there is a strong economic component to some low-income participants' opposition to migration (Chapter 6). However, Inglehart and Norris (2016) are among political scientists, as I argued in previous chapters, to categorise opposition to migration as primarily a cultural phenomenon. In doing so, and also in their categorisation of distrust of expertise as primarily a cultural phenomenon, they overplay how much more significant the 'cultural cleavage' in beliefs is than the economic one.

It is important to explore the understandings of those with higher incomes and those with many years in education as much as those with lower incomes, in order to ensure we are reflecting critically on all understandings and not assuming that those with higher incomes represent some kind of norm. In Cramer's ethnographic study she engages intensively with numerous groups of friends and workers across rural Wisconsin to reveal that their economic and cultural beliefs are entwined in a 'politics of resentment' (2016). One of the benefits of her interpretivist approach is that by asking about webs of beliefs in context, taking a holistic approach, she can gain insights into how people themselves categorise 'cultural' and 'economic' and how complex that often is. This book echoes Cramer in suggesting that participants entwine their economic and cultural reasoning. In response to questions like 'what do you understand about employment, or debt?' participants often bring in what could be called moral or cultural aspects to their beliefs. However, because in Cramer's study she does not compare the rural with the urban sector, she risks leaving the reader with the impression that it is mainly the marginalised, rural residents who express the politics of resentment and entwine the cultural and economic, and that urban ones might be doing it less. However, in this study I find that, in general, *both low-and high-income participants* entwine their cultural and economic reasoning. In their economic life stories, high-income participants relate many cultural tropes and messages, such as the importance of being frugal and prudent. In fact they are arguably more cultural, in the sense of moral, on the subject of both personal and national debt than low-income participants. Contrary to the picture of 'the economy'-obsessed Remainers in the Prosser et al. (2016) word clouds, high-income Remainers in this study are less focused on 'the economy' than might be expected, with many bringing in cultural values of internationalism to their positive understandings of migration. Arguably, there is more emphasis on 'the economy' from the low-income Remainers.

Therefore, by studying the full range of backgrounds rather than one sector, we gain a comparative perspective that helps to prevent any assumption that marginalised people might entwine moral and economic beliefs to a greater degree than high-income people do. Of course no ethnography can be representative of an entire population. This study can be criticised for taking place in only one city. Cramer could legitimately respond that if she had also researched the urban she would have lost some of the rigour of her rural fieldwork. However, there is a danger if the majority of political ethnographies are of the lower income, the rural residents, those deemed outside the circles most academic political scientists frequent. In a UK context, it is notable that less attention has been paid to Remain voters' motives than Leave voters. Ensuring we conduct some ethnographies covering a range of backgrounds may help us to reflect on how we as political scientists categorise and help us to avoid problematising the beliefs and understandings of those who have different experiences from our own.

Increasing 'dissociation' from 'the economy'

This book challenges the 'post-materialist' claim (Inglehart and Norris 2016, 2019) that 'the economy' is becoming less important to all people. It also challenges the claim in commentary on Brexit Britain that 'the economy' is becoming less important in particular to low-income people (Kaufmann 2017). Instead it backs scholarship that suggests that understandings of 'the economy' are *changing*. The interpretation low-income participants have of the 'official' economy as something that does not benefit them, and therefore that they feel dissociated from, has increased in recent years. It is this process which gives an appearance of 'the economy' becoming less important relative to culture. But if people's own understandings of 'the economy' are taken into account, it is still important to them.

'The economy' is of fundamental importance to Gary, quoted at the start of this chapter. 'The economy' means he and his partner have not been out for months, forcing them to draw on deep reserves to fight boredom and confined horizons. 'The economy' was paying them tax credits that have now been cut, meaning if one more thing goes wrong with the car they will have to scrap it, with huge repercussions for his capacity to travel to work. 'The economy' has encouraged him to undertake the course to get promotion in order to try to achieve a bit more freedom in future from 'the economy'. In ordinary talk about 'the economy' throughout this book low-income participants express strong concerns about employment (Chapter 3), debt and austerity (Chapter 4), the economic effects of migration (Chapter 5) and the effects of the financial crisis of 2008 (Chapter 6).

What low-income participants reject is not 'the economy' per se, but the version of it they have experienced in the neoliberal era. The real lived experiences of 'the economy' in recent decades, the slow recovery from 2008, the economic inequality and perceptions of 'the economy' as unfairly hitting some while it benefits the rich may have fractured the connection between 'the economy' in the aggregate and the everyday economic lives of low-income people.

Many political economists have highlighted the effects of growing inequality and stagnating recovery on political behaviour. Some argue recent governments have followed a neoliberal economics approach of attempting to put 'the economy' beyond contestation, which has further fuelled anger and disillusionment. Watson describes the depoliticisation of 'the economy' and reification of 'the market' (2018). He argues the market and 'the economy' are reified so that the humans within it are no longer perceived as having agency. But having reified the market or economy, the neoliberal approach then frames 'the economy' as an actor on the global stage. The ascription of agency is not to individuals acting in a market/economy but to the market/economy itself. In this construction, the people who have power in 'the economy' are not agents and therefore not responsible when things go wrong. In recent years, governments have attempted to present 'the economy' as having agency in order to justify the lack of any alternative to a laissez faire approach (Burnham 2001; Bourdieu 2002; Crouch 2004; Fawcett et al. 2017; Watson 2018).

These writers argue that successive governments' pursuance of depoliticisation strategies which present 'the economy' as beyond contestation was always likely to cause some kind of backlash from those not benefiting from it. Low-income people are so angry with both the effects of 'the economy' on them and the attempts to depoliticise it that they increasingly reject the official discourse on it. Ethnographer Mckenzie argues working-class Leave voters felt 'fundamentally dissociated' from the Remain rhetoric to vote for the sake of 'the economy' (2017:201). Watson (2017) argues that in the UK's referendum on the EU, low-income Leave voters cared about their own economic lives, but rejected the economic arguments of Cameron and Osborne. In part their rejection was based on the two of them having been the architects of austerity, making false promises that all would share equally in the burden of it. Several years into austerity politics, low-income voters felt they had paid a disproportionate price and 'the economy' had not improved in ways that benefited them. Hence, Watson argues low-income voters rejected Osborne's calls to do what is 'best for the economy' because 'the economy is not something they feel does right by them'. The experts' fears about 'the economy' in the referendum campaign appeared to be 'speaking somebody else's language'. He echoes Mckenzie in arguing that many on low incomes were so alienated from the discourse that they voted Leave as a gamble because they could not believe their economic prospects could get any worse outside the European Union.

In Chapter 1 I outlined how while unfolding Brexit events exercise a powerful effect in their talk about 'the economy', most participants old enough to remember do refer to past events, whether the events are the 2008 crisis or the deindustrialisation and pro-market shift of the Thatcher years. In some senses, understandings of 'the economy' seem long-standing. This echoes Hopkin, who argues the 2016 Leave victory stems from long-term economic change going back to the 1980s.

> The dramatic changes brought by globalisation, the extension of market relationships to new areas of social life and the acute shock to material living standards resulting from the financial crisis could be expected to produce a powerful political counter-movement. The Brexit vote displays the characteristics of a protest against the social, economic and cultural consequences of a long process of marketisation of the British economy. (2017b:475)

This line of thinking is backed by evidence that, in effect, 'the economy' is becoming less 'valence'; the goal of a 'healthy' economy that could benefit all is less supported by all than it once was. Recent commentary on the referendum by Clarke et al. (2017:147) reflects on the common survey finding that low-income people increasingly tend to be more pessimistic about their own economies than the national one. Some political behaviour scholars think something is changing. Borges et al. note survey evidence shows 73 per cent now believe economic inequality is a serious problem in the UK. They say there are:

> Widely shared beliefs that Britain is blighted by a toxic mix of corporate greed, excessive bank profits, economic inequality and social injustice. (2013:402)

They take 'cognitive and emotional reactions to 'the economy' into account to conclude the economy is becoming less of a valence concept and more of a contested one.

> Policy positions and equity-fairness judgments are supplementing and shaping key valence factors in the skein of forces driving party support in the present era of economic crisis and austerity politics. (2013:402)

The need for more ethnographic research

We should be intent on developing methods which help us to reveal reasoning and understanding in all its forms, from the bottom up in ways that encourage us to reflect on our own understandings. Ethnographic research should sit alongside survey evidence to help reveal insights into terms used in surveys and should be extended in political behaviour, where they are currently underused. But I also argue that, on the ethnography front, we need ethnographies exploring a range of backgrounds to supplement the sectoral ones that only explore the marginalised.

This study took place in dramatic years of British political history. I noticed that as events happened they were at the foreground of people's minds to give as examples and this emphasises the historical contingency of ethnographic study. It was frustrating that I had no previous ethnographic study to compare my findings with to help me reach stronger conclusions about how understandings might have changed over time. I hope future ethnographers will be able to use this study to track changes over time and that some kind of longitudinal panel-based study could be developed.

Conclusion

This book suggests that income amounts to a fault line in understandings of 'the economy' as more or less impersonal and benign, which needs to be incorporated into analyses of where economy ends and culture begins. Where 'the economy' or 'economic' begins and ends may happen in different places for different income groups and may mask how important 'the economy' is to people.

Participants had many motives for taking part in this research, but there was a subtle difference in how low- and high-income participants viewed the *point of the research*. The purpose of the research was hard to explain in a couple of sentences on the doorstep. However, generally high-income participants were keen to take part, first, because they thought 'the economy' was an important issue and, second, because they thought it was important for the nation to gain *higher* levels of understanding about 'the economy' in order to achieve a healthier economy and polity. They wanted 'other, less educated' people to understand the needs of 'the economy' the way they did.

However, lower-income participants' motives for taking part were different. They were keen to talk, specifically *so their voices could be heard by politicians and others*. In the case of Leave voters, or those opposed to migration, there was an extra edge because they wanted to explain they were not racist or stupid. However, generally, lower-income participants felt they had a duty to educate experts and others who were not in touch with their economic conditions. For the higher-income participants, the motive was to enhance a pre-existing and taken-for-granted 'economy'. For the lower income participants, the motive was to take part in a discussion about 'the rigged economy' they felt other people did not understand.

Appendix

Recruiting participants from a range of backgrounds

Here I give more details about how I recruited to ensure participants were from a range of backgrounds and what the backgrounds were.

As I discussed in previous chapters, interpretivists do not assume people's beliefs will correspond to pre-defined social categories. Nevertheless, I believed it was important to try to recruit from people with a wide variety of economic experiences and also ages. So I adopted a 'sample frame approach' to recruiting (Ritchie et al. 2014:chapter 5) using a rough grid of the proportions of age, gender and occupational groups spread across southern England. The grid gave me very approximate guidelines such as to recruit 50 per cent women, 40 per cent from occupational groups A and B, 60 per cent from occupational groups C1–E and rough proportions from each age group. When I found I was recruiting too many over-sixties, because they had time available, I amended the invitation in the next street to include participants from eighteen to sixty only. When I needed to recruit extra women, I asked men on the doorstep if I could talk to any women living in the house and was open about the fact that not so many women had so far stepped forward. I gave some details of the range of backgrounds participants came from in Chapter 2, but give more details here.

Occupation

The occupational groupings I use throughout this book are based on the six class Socio-Economic Classifications set out in Table A.1.[1]

I did not start the interview with questions about occupational background. When I did ask a few how they thought they fitted into the SEC categories above they were unsure. However, so much of the interview was about what work participants had done, or in the case of eighteen-year-olds what work their parents

---

[1] This is a well established measure of occupation; further details are available at, for instance, www.ukgeographics.co.uk/blog/social-grade-a-b-c1-c2-d-e.

Table A.1 SEC occupational groupings

Social grade	Description
AB	Higher and intermediate managerial, administrative, professional occupations
C1	Supervisory, clerical and junior managerial, administrative, professional occupations
C2	Skilled manual occupations
DE	Semi-skilled and unskilled manual occupations, Unemployed and lowest-grade occupations

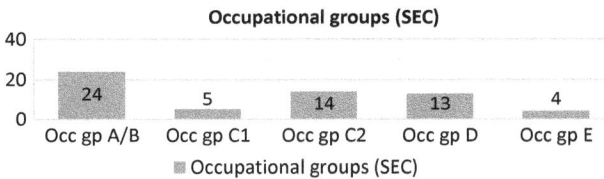

Figure A.1 Participants' occupational categories

did, that I was able to assess which occupational category they fitted. I was able to make a more informed judgement about their occupational background than if conducting a survey with perhaps just one question about current occupation. Taking the two districts together, thirty-six participants fit occupational groups C, D, E and twenty-four fit occupational groups A and B, as shown in Figure A.1.

I do not want to list specific occupations next to each name in case it compromises anonymity, but I present them in Table A.2 in aggregate, broken into private and public sector. Where the participant was retired I use their most recent occupation.

Gender

Twenty-eight participants were women and thirty-two were men.

Age

The age spread of participants is set out in Figure A.2.

Ethnicity/nationality

I made efforts to seek out participants from the range of nationalities and ethnic backgrounds in the city. Two Polish women agreed to take part and, where

Table A.2 Participants' current and former occupations

Hill district domestic/ benefits	Four carers, one foster carer
Hill district private sector	Four drivers (taxi or fork lift), four factory, two catering, two administrative assistants, one mechanic, one landscape gardener, one charity, one cleaner
Hill district public sector	Two education, five health workers or technicians, one administrative (finance), one university student
Church district private	One property manager, one executive manufacturing, one engineer, one ICT senior manager, one estate agent assistant, one bank, one ICT
Church district public	Five health, four education, one university librarian
Out-of-district private	Two accountants/finance, one researcher
Out-of-district public	Eight college students, one trade union manager, one nurse

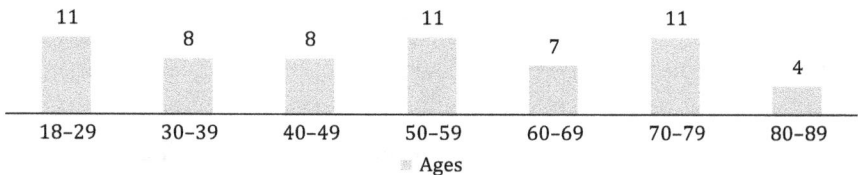

Figure A.2 Participants' age distribution

relevant, I refer to this when presenting their beliefs. Seven participants were from black and ethnic minority backgrounds. The number of BAME and non-UK-born participants was small so I am reluctant to identify trends that might relate to ethnicity or nationality; follow-up research needs to be conducted to explore this subject further.

Political affiliation

The general election vote is set out in Figure A.3. The 2016 referendum vote breaks down as shown below. A majority were Remain voters, although the city as a whole voted Leave. I comment more in Chapter 2 about non-voters. We should remember that general election and referendum turnout are still usually only about 70 per cent, so that the high number of non-voters, once eighteen-year-olds or EU citizens not eligible to vote is taken into account, is not unusual.

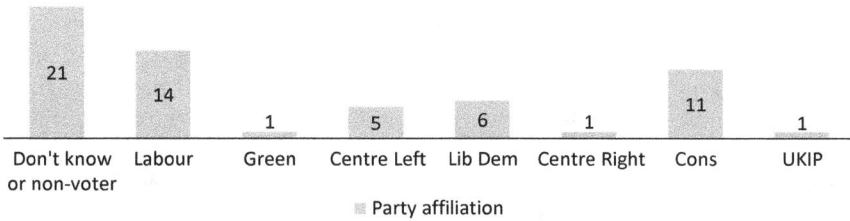

Figure A.3 Participants' general election vote

Figure A.4 Participants' 2016 referendum vote

Honoraria

I offered an honorarium of £10 for an interview and £20 for taking part in a focus group. There is a debate about whether to give honoraria (for a review, see Cheff 2018). I agreed with the conclusions of Cheff that it was important to show respect for the time participants were giving up. Some refused the honorarium. It is impossible to tell how much the honorarium was an incentive to take part.

Anonymisation

How did protection of anonymity work in practice? The participation information and consent forms made it clear I would use their words but that I would apply a pseudonym and change-distinguishing features, such as very distinctive life experiences. I adopted the Braun and Clarke option of replacing specific information with generic descriptions (2013:166, 169).

An additional problem was how to provide 'humanising details' about each participant quoted so the reader could become familiar with them and the ethnography read more like thick description or, as Madden defines it, 'storied reality' (2017:16). It is particularly hard for the reader to feel familiar when, as in this case, there were sixty participants. However, humanising might lead to stereotyping. For instance, Misha was a single parent in her thirties, trained as a teaching assistant although not able to work due to one of her children's conditions. What key aspects of her personality and story 'humanise' her? She was intelligent, honest, outrageous sometimes, and tended to see both sides of the picture. Calling her a 'single parent on benefits in her early thirties' throughout would not humanise her. But how could I remind readers which participant she was in her second or third quotes? If I varied the humanising details depending on the quote, so for instance it was relevant to one quote that, as she said, she was the mixed-race child of a Jamaican father and white British mother, but in another quote far more relevant that she was a single parent struggling on a low income, then did such disparate descriptions of her help the reader? There was no easy answer to this and I did the best I could, with sensitivity to the participants foremost in my mind.

Thematic analysis

Thematic analysis as described by Braun and Clarke (2006, 2013) is a flexible but rigorous approach to coding transcripts used in psychology and the social sciences more widely. Braun and Clarke describe the lengthy process of coding in Table A.3. The codes and themes are not pre-defined, but emerge from reading and re-reading transcripts.

Braun and Clarke (2006) set out a fifteen-point checklist, in Table A.4, to ensure rigorous thematic analysis, which I use at the end of the process, to meet the criterion that the research is an accurate interpretation of participants' words.

Table A.3 Stages in thematic analysis

1	Familiarise yourself with the data, read many times and jot notes.
2	Generate initial codes – these identify semantic or latent features that appear interesting.
3	Search for themes – sort the codes into themes.
4	Review themes – they should be internally homogeneous and externally heterogeneous. The researcher may have to move or discard themes, make a map of entire data set to check themes are accurate.
5	Define and name themes and sub-themes, writing detailed analyses for each, the story the themes tell and how they fit with the broader story the data set tells.
6	Write up giving a precise account of the story the data will tell within and across themes, using as much thick description as possible.

Adapted from Braun and Clarke (2013:202).

Table A.4 Quality criteria checklist for thematic analysis

Stage	Quality criteria checklist
Transcription	1 The data have been transcribed to an appropriate level of detail, and the transcripts have been checked against the tapes for 'accuracy'.
Coding	2 Each data item has been given equal attention in the coding process.
	3 Themes have not been generated from a few vivid examples (an anecdotal approach), but instead the coding process has been thorough, inclusive and comprehensive.
	4 All relevant extracts for all each theme have been collated.
	5 Themes have been checked against each other and back to the original data set.
	6 Themes are internally coherent, consistent and distinctive.
Analysis	7 Data have been analysed – interpreted, made sense of – rather than just paraphrased or described.
	8 Analysis and data match each other – the extracts illustrate the analytic claims.
	9 Analysis tells a convincing and well-organised story about the data and topic.
	10 A good balance between analytic narrative and illustrative extracts is provided.
Overall	11 Enough time has been allocated to complete all phases of the analysis adequately, without rushing a phase or giving it a once-over-lightly.
Written report	12 The assumptions about, and specific approach to, thematic analysis are clearly explicated.
	13 There is a good fit between what you claim you do, and what you show you have done – i.e., described method and reported analysis are consistent.
	14 The language and concepts position of the analysis used in the report are consistent with the epistemological approach.
	15 The researcher is positioned as active in the research process; themes do not just 'emerge'.

Adapted from Braun and Clarke (2006:36).

Interview and focus group guides

Interview guide[2]

ARRIVAL: time available, place.

PRE-INTERVIEW: consent form purpose of research, publication of research (confidentiality). There are no right answers, don't answer any you feel uncomfortable about.

---

[2] In semi-structured interviewing such as in this study, question sequencing and exact wording varied.

DURING INTERVIEW: age, employment, household composition, education (have you ever been taught anything about politics or economics?), political affiliation if any.

In-depth interview/discussion topic areas

Approach to money/provisioning on a personal level

1. Going back to your childhood, how were you provided for? [Subsequent possible prompts: what kinds of jobs did your parents have? Did they own their own house? Would you describe your childhood as comfortably off? Do you remember them having financial pressures? Did your parents talk about them?]
2. How have you provided for yourself as an adult? [Subsequent possible prompts: what jobs, housing, financial pressures etc.?]
3. What/how much do you feel you know/understand about money and your household economy?

Beliefs about 'economic' and 'economy'

4. During your life have you been aware of 'the economy' affecting you?
5. How do you define 'the economy?' [Subsequent possible prompts: thinking about the national economy, what words or images spring to mind when the word 'economy' is mentioned? If the news presenter says 'coming up on the lunch-time news today we will be hearing from our economics correspondent', what is your gut feeling? Why? Could you say more?]
6. Thinking about your understanding, where would you say it MOSTLY comes from [if prompts needed, e.g., friends and family, politicians, media, life experience?] Question newspapers read, relevant TV and internet sources used and whether they talk about the national economy much in the course of everyday life.
7. Who do you think economic experts are? What do you believe about economic expertise?

Understanding of key components of economy

8. What do you understand about each of these? Give as cards, encourage as much talk as possible including about related policy and only ask probing questions, don't give answers.

- Inflation   • Employment   • Trade
- Debt/deficit (include probing of household analogy)   • Banks
- Gov't spending   • Taxation
- Migration (include probing questions on economic information during EU referendum campaign and how they voted and how economic they think their vote was)

9. Final question: How much (in your own words) do you feel you understand about 'the economy'? Is there anything else you would like to say that you think is relevant?

Focus group guide[3]

As they come in, participation form and consent form.

Introduction

Remember me, introduce my assistant.

This is a focus group; there are different kinds of focus groups. This is academic, qualitative, I have interviewed sixty people, hope to conduct focus groups with twenty of those – subject is public understanding of the economy.

Purpose of the focus group.

- Questions have cropped up from the interviews and maybe if you talked about them in a group it might help me answer them.
- Also I would appreciate feedback on my main conclusion second half of the focus group.

Introductions; name cards.

Ground rules:

- there is no right or wrong
- respect
- don't talk over one another to confuse the tape
- if you need a comfort break or want to withdraw, get up and go.

Starting questions – defining economy

1. How do you define 'the economy'?
2. How close do you feel to 'the economy'?

[3] In semi-structured focus groups such as in this study, question sequencing and exact wording varied.

3. Are these economic issues? [Use cards from interviews]

- employment
- trade
- inflation
- taxation
- government spending
- debt
- banking

4. What other important issues would you add?

Is migration an economic issue?

5. How economic was your vote in the 2016 referendum?

How positive are you about 'the economy' and economic experts?

6. How positive do you feel about the word 'economy' or 'economic'?
7. Who are the economic experts?
8. Which do you trust?

Here are my findings, what do you think?

- Most people's understanding of the economy is based on personal experience.
- Understanding of the economy varies with income; higher-income people may interact with the economy in *more* ways but do not necessarily have a deeper understanding of it.
- Higher-income people are more positive about 'the economy' and use the term more often.

Closing

Did you have any other thoughts on the economy you wanted to share?
What has it felt like to participate in this focus group?
Thanks and follow-up draft report summary at some point.
Please let me know if you would like to claim expenses.

References

Agar, M. and Macdonald, J. (1995). 'Focus groups and ethnography'. *Human Organization*, 54:1, 78–86.

Alesina, A. and Ferrera, E. (2002). 'Who trusts others?' *Journal of Public Economics*, 85:2, 207–34.

Bartlett, N. (2017) 'Labour will not put up income tax for those earning less than £80,000'. *Mirror*, 6 May 2017.

Bazerman, M., Baron, J. and Shonk, K. (2001). *You Can't Enlarge the Pie: Six Barriers to Effective Government*. New York: Basic Books.

Bell, T. (2016). 'The referendum, living standards and inequality.' Blog, Resolution Foundation. Accessed 3 February 2019. www.resolutionfoundation.org/media/blog/the-referendum-living-standards-and-inequality/.

Bennett, R. and Kottasz, R. (2012). 'Public attitudes towards the UK banking industry following the global financial crisis'. *International Journal of Bank Marketing*, 30:2, 128–47.

Berger, P. and Luckmann, T. (1971). *The Social Construction of Reality: A Treatise in the Sociology of Knowledge*. Harmondsworth: Penguin.

Berry, C (2016). 'How austerity took Britain to Brexit.' Blog, The UK in a changing Europe. Accessed 2 January 2017. http://ukandeu.ac.uk/how-austerity-took-britain-to-brexit/Berry C.

Best, J. and Paterson, M. (2010). 'Understanding political economy'. In Best, J. and Paterson, M. (eds), *Cultural Political Economy*. London: Routledge.

Bevir, M. and Rhodes, R.A.W. (2015). *Routledge Handbook of Interpretive Political Science*. Abingdon: Routledge.

Blinder, A. and Krueger, A. (2004). 'What does the public know about economic policy, and how does it know it?' *Brookings Papers on Economic Activity* 1, 327–97.

Blinder, S. (2015). 'Imagined immigration: the impact of different meanings of "immigrants" in public opinion and policy debates in Britain'. *Political Studies*, 63:1, 80–100.

Blyth, M. (2013). *Austerity: The History of a Dangerous Idea*. New York: Oxford University Press.

Borges, W., Clarke, H., Stewart, M., Sanders, D. and Whiteley, P. (2013). 'The emerging political economy of austerity in Britain'. *Electoral Studies*, 32:3, 396–403.

Boswell, J., Denham, J., Furlong, J., Killick, A., Ndugga, P., Rek, B., Ryan, M. and Shipp, J. (2018). *Making Ends Meet: The Lived Experience of Poverty in the South.* Southampton: Southern Policy Centre and Joseph Rowntree Foundation.

Bourdieu, P. (2002). 'Against the policy of depoliticization'. *Studies in Political Economy*, 69:1, 31–41.

Braun, V. and Clarke, V. (2006). 'Using thematic analysis in psychology'. *Qualitative Research in Psychology*, 3:2, 77–101.

Braun, V. and Clarke, V. (2013). *Successful Qualitative Research.* London: Sage.

British Election Study (BES) (2017). 'Face to face survey questionnaire.' Accessed 2 January 2018. http://britishelectionstudy.com/wp-content/uploads/2018/01/BES-2017-F2F-codebook.pdf.

Brückner, S., Förster, M., Zlatkin-Troitschanskaia, O., Happ, R., Walstad, W., Yamaoka, M. and Asano, T. (2015). 'Gender effects in assessment of economic knowledge and understanding: differences among undergraduate business and economics students in Germany, Japan, and the United States'. *Peabody Journal of Education*, 90:4, 503–18.

Burnham, P. (2001). 'New Labour and the politics of depoliticisation'. *British Journal of Politics and International Relations*, 3:2, 127–49.

Campbell, A. and Converse P. (1960). *The American Voter.* New York: John Wiley & Sons.

Caplan, B. (2001). 'What makes people think like economists? Evidence on economic cognition from the "Survey of Americans and Economists on the Economy".' *Journal of Law & Economics*, 44:2, 395–426.

Caplan, B. (2002). 'Systematically biased beliefs about economics: robust evidence of judgemental anomalies from the survey of Americans and economists on the economy.' *The Economic Journal*, 112:479, 433–58.

Caplan, B. (2008). *The Myth of the Rational Voter: Why Democracies Choose Bad Policies (New Edition).* Princeton, NJ: Princeton University Press.

Cheff, R. (2018). 'Compensating research participants: a review of current practices in Toronto'. Wellesley Institute Report. Accessed 9 February 2019 https://wellesleyinstitute.com/wp-content/uploads/2018/07/Fair-compensation-Report-.pdf.

Clark, K., Drinkwater, S., Eade, J. and Garapich, M. (2017). 'EU migration and the transformation of the UK labour market in the twenty-first century.' Paper for Department of Work and Pensions Economics Group Annual Conference, Sheffield, July 2017. Accessed 6 June 2019. www.sheffield.ac.uk/polopoly_fs/1.735893!/file/E2_1_Drinkwater.pdf.

Clarke, H., Goodwin, M. and Whiteley, P. (2017). *Brexit: Why Britain Voted to Leave the European Union.* Cambridge: Cambridge University Press.

Colantone, I. and Stanig, P. (2016). 'Global competition and Brexit'. *BAFFI CAREFIN Centre Research Paper*, Series number 2016–44.

Cramer, K. (2016). *The Politics of Resentment: Rural Consciousness in Wisconsin and the Rise of Scott Walker.* Chicago: University of Chicago Press.

Cramer, K. and Toff, B. (2017). 'The fact of experience: rethinking political knowledge and civic competence'. *Perspectives on Politics*, 15:3, 754–70.

Crewe, E. (2015). *The House of Commons: An Anthropology of MPs at Work.* London: Bloomsbury Academic.

Crouch, C. (2004). *Post-Democracy.* Cambridge: Polity.

Curtice, J. (2016). 'The two poles of the referendum debate: immigration and the economy.' London: NatCen Social Research. Accessed 6 July 2017. https://whatukthinks.org/eu/wp-content/uploads/2016/01/Analysis-paper-4-The-two-poles-of-the-referendum-debate.pdf.

Dathan, M. (2016). 'David Cameron mocks Nigel Farage for the way he pronounces his "poncey, foreign-sounding" name'. *MailOnline*. 27 April 2016. Accessed 8 July 2017. https://dailymail.co.uk/news/article-3561564/David-Cameron-mocks-Nigel-Farage-way-pronounces-poncey-foreign-sounding-name.html.

Dhingra, S., Ottaviano, G., Sampson, T. and Van Reenen, J. (2016). 'Brexit and the impact of immigration on the UK in performance'. In Centre for Economic Performance (ed.), *Brexit 2016: Policy Analysis from the Centre for Economic Performance*. London: LSE.

Doherty, M. (2016). 'Through the looking glass: Brexit, free movement and the future'. *King's Law Journal*, 27:3, 375–86.

Dorling, D. (2016). 'Brexit: the decision of a divided country.' *British Medical Journal*, 354:i3697.

Duch, R. and Stevenson, R. (2008). *The Economic Vote: How Political and Economic Institutions Condition Election Results. Political Economy of Institutions and Decisions.* Cambridge: Cambridge University Press.

Dustmann, C., Frattini, T. and Preston, I. (2008). 'The effect of immigration along the distribution of wages'. Centre for Research and Analysis of Migration, Discussion paper series (CDP No 03/08).

Dustmann, C. and Frattini, T. (2014). 'The fiscal effects of immigration to the UK'. *The Economic Journal*, 124:580, 593–643.

Earle, J., Moran, C. and Ward Perkins, Z. (2017). *The Econocracy: The Perils of Leaving Economics to the Experts*. Manchester: Manchester University Press.

Edelman Trust (2017). 'Edelman Trust barometer annual global study UK findings'. Accessed 6 June 2018. https://edelman.co.uk/magazine/posts/edelman-trust-barometer-2017-uk-findings/.

Fawcett, P., Flinders, M., Hay, C. and Wood, M. (2017). *Anti-Politics, Depoliticization, and Governance*. Oxford: Oxford University Press.

Ferber, M., Birnbaum, B. and Green, C. (1983). 'Gender differences in economic knowledge: a re-evaluation of the evidence'. *The Journal of Economic Education*, 14:2, 24–37.

Ferber, M. and Nelson, J.A. (2003). *Feminist Economics Today: Beyond Economic Man*. Chicago: University of Chicago Press.

Ford, R. (2011). 'Acceptable and unacceptable immigrants: the ethnic hierarchy in British immigration preferences'. *Journal of Ethnic and Migration Studies*, 37:7, 1017–37.

Ford, R. and Lymperopoulou, K. (2017). 'Immigration: how attitudes in the UK compare with Europe'. British Social Attitudes 34. Accessed 6 January 2018. http://bsa.natcen.ac.uk/media/39148/bsa34_immigration_final.pdf.

Frank, T. (2007). *What's the Matter with Kansas? How the Conservatives won the Heart of America*. New York: Henry Holt and Company.

Gamble, A. (2013). 'Neo-liberalism and fiscal conservatism'. In Schmidt, V. and Thatcher, M. (eds), *Resilient Liberalism in Europe's Political Economy*. Cambridge: Cambridge University Press.

Gamson, W. (1992). *Talking Politics*. Cambridge: Cambridge University Press.

Gangl, K., Kastlunger, B., Kirchler, E. and Voracek, M. (2012). 'Confidence in the economy in times of crisis: social representations of experts and laypeople'. *The Journal of Socio-Economics*, 41:5, 603–14.

Graeber, D. (2012). *Debt: The First 5000 Years*. New York: Melville House.

Haferkamp, A., Fetchenhauer, D., Belschak, F. and Enste, D. (2009). 'Efficiency versus fairness: the evaluation of labor market policies by economists and laypeople'. *Journal of Economic Psychology*, 30:4, 527–39.

Hammond, P. (2016). Speech to Conservative Party Conference. Accessed 6 June 2018. https://politicshome.com/news/uk/economy/economic-growth/news/79538/read-philip-hammonds-full-speech-tory-party-conference.

Hann, C. and Hart, K. (2011). *Economic Anthropology*. Bristol: Polity.

Hay, C. (2010). 'Chronicles of a death foretold: the winter of discontent and construction of the crisis of British Keynesianism'. *Parliamentary Affairs*, 63:3, 446–70.

Hobolt, S., Leeper, T. and Tilley, J. (2018). 'Emerging Brexit identities'. Blog, The UK in a Changing Europe. Accessed 6 February 2019. https://ukandeu.ac.uk/emerging-brexit-identities/.

Hopkin, J. (2017a). 'The Brexit vote and general election were both about austerity and inequality'. LSE Brexit blog. Accessed 6 February 2018. http://blogs.lse.ac.uk/brexit/2017/06/28/the-brexit-vote-and-general-election-were-both-about-austerity-and-inequality/.

Hopkin, J. (2017b). 'When Polanyi met Farage: market fundamentalism, economic nationalism, and Britain's exit from the European Union'. *The British Journal of Politics and International Relations*, 19:3, 465–78.

Inglehart, R. and Norris, N. (2016). 'Trump, Brexit and the rise of populism: economic have-nots and cultural backlash'. Harvard Kennedy School Working Paper RWP16–026.

Inglehart, R. and Norris, N. (2019). *Cultural Backlash and the Rise of Populism: Trump, Brexit, and Authoritarian Populism*. Cambridge: Cambridge University Press.

Independent Television (ITV) (2019). 'Labour to push for second Brexit referendum after meaningful vote'. Report, 27 February at 10:38pm. https://itv.com/news/2019-02-27/labour-to-push-for-second-brexit-referendum-after-meaningful-vote-john-mcdonnell/.

Jaumotte, F., Koloskova, K. and Saxena, S. (2016). 'Migrants bring economic benefits for advanced economies'. Blog, International Monetary Fund. Accessed 6 February 2017. https://blogs.imf.org/2016/10/24/migrants-bring-economic-benefits-for-advanced-economies/9.

Kaufmann, E. (2017). 'Values and immigration – the real reasons behind Brexit and Trump'. In Mair, J. (ed.), *Brexit, Trump and the Media*. Bury St Edmunds: Abramis.

Kaufmann, E. (2018). 'Why culture is more important than skills in understanding British public opinion on immigration'. Blog, LSE Politics and Policy, 30 January. Accessed 6 February 2018. http://blogs.lse.ac.uk/politicsandpolicy/why-culture-is-more-important-than-skills-understanding-british-public-opinion-on-immigration/.

Killick, A. (2017a). 'Do people really lack knowledge about the economy? A reply to Facchini.' *Political Quarterly*, 88:2, 265–72.

Killick, A. (2017b). 'Education or knowledge? We need to rethink how we measure people's understanding of politics'. LSE blog, British Politics and Policy. Accessed 26 August 2019. https://blogs.lse.ac.uk/politicsandpolicy/education-or-knowledge-measuring-public-knowledge/.

Kroknes, V., Jakobsen, T. and Grønning, L. (2015). 'Economic performance and political trust: the impact of the financial crisis on European citizens'. *European Societies*, 17:5, 700–23.

Lane R. (1962). *Political Ideology: Why the American Common Man Believes What He Does*. New York: Free Press of Glencoe.

Legrain, P. (no date). 'Brexit: an act of economic self harm'. Accessed 8 December 2018. http://clubofthree.org/brexit-an-act-of-economic-self-harm/.

Leiser, D., Bourgeois-Gironde, S. and Benita, R. (2010). 'Human foibles or systemic failure – lay perceptions of the 2008–2009 financial crisis'. *The Journal of Socio-Economics*, 39:2, 132–41.

Lewis-Beck, M., Nadeau, R. and Foucault, M. (2012). 'The compleat economic voter: new theory and British evidence'. *British Journal of Political Science*, 43:2, 241–61.

Lewis-Beck, M., Martini, N. and Kiewiet, D. (2013). 'The nature of economic perceptions in mass publics'. *Electoral Studies*, 32:3, 524–8.

Li, Y., Pickles, A. and Savage, M. (2005). 'Social capital and social trust in Britain'. *European Sociological Review*, 21:2, 109–23.

Lippmann, W. (1922). *Public Opinion*. New York: Free Press.

Lomasky, L. (2008). 'Swing and a myth: a review of Caplan's "The Myth of the Rational Voter"'. *Public Choice*, 135:3, 469–84.

McDonnell, J. (2017). 'Andrew Marr questions John McDonnell on Marxism'. The Andrew Marr Show, BBC. 7 May 2017. Accessed 6 February 2019. https://bbc.co.uk/news/av/uk-politics-39835429/andrew-marr-questions-john-mcdonnell-on-marxism.

McDonnell, A. and Curtis, C. (2019). 'How Britain voted in the 2019 general election'. YouGov. Accessed 2 January 2019. https://yougov.co.uk/topics/politics/articles-reports/2019/12/17/how-britain-voted-2019-general-election.

Mckenzie, L. (2017). '"It's not ideal": reconsidering "anger" and "apathy" in the Brexit vote among an invisible working class'. *Competition and Change*, 21:3, 199–210.

McLaren, L. and Johnson, M. (2007). 'Resources, group conflict and symbols: explaining anti-immigration hostility in Britain'. *Political Studies*, 55:4, 709–32.

Madden, R. (2017). *Being Ethnographic*. London: Sage.

Mitchell, T. (1998). 'Fixing the economy'. *Cultural Studies*, 12:1, 82–101.

Mitchell, T. (2008a). 'Rethinking economy'. *Geoforum*, 39:3, 1116–21.

Mitchell, T. (2008b). 'Culture and economy'. In Bennett, T. and Frow, J. (eds), *The SAGE Handbook of Cultural Analysis*. London: SAGE Publications.

Moore, M. and Ramsay, G. (2017). 'UK media coverage of the 2016 EU referendum campaign'. Centre for the Study of Media, Communication and Power: The Policy Institute at King's College London. Accessed 6 February 2018. https://kcl.ac.uk/policy-institute/assets/cmcp/uk-media-coverage-of-the-2016-eu-referendum-campaign.pdf.

Moscovici, S. (1988). 'Notes towards a description of social representations'. *European Journal of Social Psychology*, 18, 211–50.

New Economic Foundation (NEF) (2018). *Framing the Economy*. London: New Economy Organisers' Network (NEON), NEF, Frameworks Institute, Public Interest Research Centre. Accessed 7 November 2018. http://neweconomics.org/wp-content/uploads/2018/02/Framing-the-Economy-NEON-NEF-FrameWorks-PIRC.pdf.

Nickell, S. and Saleheen, J. (2015). 'The impact of immigration on occupational wages: evidence from Britain'. Bank of England Staff Working Paper 574.

Norrish, A. (2017). 'Exploring how people feel about economics'. Economy.org. Accessed 6 November 2017. https://ecnmy.org/research/report-2017/.

O'Connor, C. (2012). 'Using social representations theory to examine lay explanation of contemporary social crises: the case of Ireland's recession'. *Journal of Community and Applied Social Psychology*, 22:6, 453–69.

Organisation for Economic Co-operation and Development (OECD) (2014). 'Migration policy debates'. Accessed 6 February 2017. https://oecd.org/migration/OECD%20Migration%20Policy%20Debates%20Numero%202.pdf.

Osborne, G. (2010). Full-text Chancellor's speech to Conservative Party Conference. Accessed 6 February 2017. https://theguardian.com/politics/2010/oct/04/george-osborne-speech-conservative-conference.

Owen, E. and Walter, S. (2017). 'Open economy politics and Brexit: insights puzzles and ways forward' *Review of International Political Economy*, 24:2, 179–202.

Pader, E. (2006). 'Seeing with an ethnographic sensibility: explorations beneath the surface of public policies'. In Yanow, D. and Schwartz-Shea, P. (eds), *Interpretation and Method: Empirical Research Methods and the Interpretive Turn*. Armonk, NY: M.E. Sharpe, Inc.

Park, Y. and Kim, Y. (2018). 'Explaining the Brexit referendum: the role of worker skill level in voter decisions'. *The Political Quarterly*, 89:4, 640–8.

Pilkington, H. (2016). *Loud and Proud: Passion and Politics in the English Defence League*. Manchester: Manchester University Press.

Polanyi, K. (1978). *The Livelihood of Man* (Pearson, H. (ed.)). New York: Academic Press Inc.

Polanyi, K. (2001). *The Great Transformation: The Political and Economic Origins of Our Time*, 2nd edn. Boston: Beacon Press.

Populus (2016). 'What will it take to restore trust in capitalism?' Opinion. Accessed 6 January 2020. www.populus.co.uk/insights/2016/04/what-will-it-take-to-restore-trust-in-capitalism/.

Power, M. (2004). 'Social provisioning as a starting point for feminist economics'. *Feminist Economics*, 10:3, 3–19.

Prosser, C., Mellon, J. and Green, J. (2016). 'What mattered most to you when deciding how to vote in the EU referendum?' British Election Studies. Accessed 6 February 2017. http://britishelectionstudy.com/bes-findings/what-mattered-most-to-you-when-deciding-how-to-vote-in-the-eu-referendum/#.WRlwe8a1uUk.

Rhodes, R.A.W. (2016). 'Local knowledge, an interpretive analysis'. In Bevir, M. and Rhodes, R.A.W. (eds), *Rethinking Governance: Ruling, Rationalities and Resistance*. Abingdon: Routledge, Studies in Governance and Public Policy.

Rhodes, R.A.W. (2017). *Interpretive Political Science: Selected Essays*, Volume II. Oxford: Oxford University Press.

Ricardo, D. [1817] (1996). *Principles of Political Economy and Taxation*. Amherst, NY: Prometheus.

Ritchie, J., Lewis, J., Elam, G., Tennant, R. and Rahim, N. (2014). *Qualitative Research Practice: A Guide for Social Science Students*. London: Sage.

Roland-Levy, C., Kirchler, E., Penz, E. and Gray, C. (eds) (2001). *Everyday Representations of the Economy*. Vienna: WUV Universitätsverlag.

Rolphe, H. (2016). 'Flexible friends: why employers hire eastern European migrants in order to grow'. LSE Brexit blog, 15 June. Accessed 6 February 2017. https://blogs.lse.ac.uk/brexit/2016/06/15/flexible-friends-why-employers-hire-eastern-european-migrants-in-order-to-grow/.

Runciman, D. (2016). 'How the education gap is tearing politics apart'. *Guardian*, 5 October. Accessed 6 November 2017. https://theguardian.com/politics/2016/oct/05/trump-brexit-education-gap-tearing-politics-apart.

Runciman, D. (2017). 'Nobody knows anything: why is politics so surprising?' Lecture: Annual Political Quarterly Lecture. Accessed 3 January 2018. http://politicalquarterly.org.uk/2017/12/the-pq-annual-lecture-by-david-runciman.html.

Sandelowski, M. (2001). 'Real qualitative researchers do not count: the use of numbers in qualitative research'. *Research in Nursing and Health*, 24, 230–40.

Sandelowski, M. (2004). 'Using qualitative research'. *Qualitative Health Research*, 14:10, 1366–86.

Schwartz-Shea, P. and Yanow, D. (2012). *Interpretive Research Design*. New York: Routledge.

Settle, M. (2016). 'Osborne: IMF warning a taste of the future after Brexit vote'. *The Herald (Glasgow)*, 13 April.

Skey, M. (2011). *National Belonging and Everyday Life: The Significance of Nationhood in an Uncertain World*. Basingstoke: Palgrave Macmillan.

Smith, A. (1999). *The Theory of Moral Sentiments*. Washington, DC: Regnery Pub.

Smith, A. and Skinner, A. (2000). *The Wealth of Nations*. London: Penguin.

Standing, G. (2011). *The Precariat: The New Dangerous Class*. London: Bloomsbury.

Stanley, L. (2014). ' "We're reaping what we sowed": everyday crisis narratives and acquiescence to the age of austerity'. *New Political Economy*, 19:6, 895–917.

Stiglitz, J., Sen, A. and Fitoussi, J-P. (2010). *Mismeasuring Our Lives: Why GDP Doesn't Add Up: The Report by the Commission on the Measurement of Economic Performance and Social Progress*. New York: The New Press.

Stokes, D. (1992). 'Valence politics'. In Kavanagh, P., Kavanagh, D. and Butler, D. (eds), *Electoral Politics*. Oxford: Clarendon Press.

Surridge, P. (2016). 'Education and liberalism: pursuing the link'. *Oxford Review of Education*, 42:2, 146–64.

Swinford, S. (2016). 'Jeremy Corbyn: there is no "upper limit" to EU migration'. *Telegraph*, 20 June.

Thomson, A. and Syvester, R. (2019). 'Greg Clarke interview: "No-deal Brexit would be a disaster something that we'd regret forever"'. *The Times*, 2 February. Accessed 6 November 2019. https://thetimes.co.uk/article/greg-clark-interview-no-deal-brexit-would-be-a-disaster-something-that-we-d-regret-for-ever-d0bcq9jgw.

Tomlinson, J. (2017). *Managing the Economy, Managing the People: Narratives of Economic Life in Britain from Beveridge to Brexit*. Oxford: Oxford University Press.

Tonkiss, K. (2016). 'Experiencing transnationalism at home: open borders and the everyday narratives of non-migrants'. *Politics*, 36:3, 324–35.

Tooze, A. (1998). 'Imagining national economies'. In Cubitt, G. (eds), *Imagining Nations*. Manchester: Manchester University Press.

Torcal, M. (2014). 'The decline of political trust in Spain and Portugal'. *American Behavioral Scientist*, 58:12, 1542–67.

UK Government (2018). 'EU exit: long-term economic analysis'. November, CM 9742. Accessed 3 January 2019. https://assets.publishing.service.gov.uk/government/uploads/system/uploads/attachment_data/file/760484/28_November_EU_Exit_-_Long-term_economic_analysis__1_.pdf.

Walstad, W. and Larsen, M. (1992). *A National Survey of American Economic Literacy*. Lincoln, NE: The Gallup Organization.

Walstad, W. and Rebeck, K. (2002). 'Assessing the economic knowledge and economic opinions of adults'. *Quarterly Review of Economics and Finance*, 42:5, 921–35.

Watson, M. (2005). *Foundations of International Political Economy*. Basingstoke: Palgrave Macmillan.

Watson, M. (2012). 'The eighteenth-century historiographic tradition and contemporary "Everyday IPE"'. *Review of International Studies*, 39:1, 1–23.

Watson, M. (2017). 'Brexit, the left behind and the let down: the political abstraction of "the economy" and the UK's EU referendum'. *British Politics*, 13:1, 17–30.

Watson, M. (2018). *The Market*. Newcastle: Agenda Publishing.

Wilkinson, M. (2016). 'Philip Hammond warns Britain's economy heading for post-Brexit "rollercoaster" ride as he drops pledge for budget surplus by 2020'. *Telegraph*, 3 October.

Williamson, M. and Wearing, A. (1996). 'Lay people's cognitive models of the economy'. *Economic Psychology*, 17:1, 3–38.

Wong, C. (2007). '"Little" and "big" pictures in our heads: race, local context, and innumeracy about racial groups in the United States'. *Public Opinion Quarterly*, 71:3, 392–412.

Wright, D. and Case, R. (2016). 'Leave voters felt ignored and left behind as post-Brexit poll reveals extent of economic division across UK'. Joseph Rowntree Foundation. Accessed 6 February 2017. https://jrf.org.uk/press/leave-voters-felt-ignored-and-left-behind-post-brexit-poll-reveals-extent-economic-division.

Wroe, A. (2014). 'Political trust and job insecurity in 18 European polities'. *Journal of Trust Research*, 4:2, 90–112.

Wroe, A. (2015). 'Economic insecurity and political trust in the United States'. *American Politics Research*, 44:1, 131–63.

Zelizer, V. (2010). *Economic Lives: How Culture Shapes the Economy*. Princeton, NJ: Princeton University Press.

Index

EU authorised representative for GPSR:
Easy Access System Europe, Mustamäe tee 50,
10621 Tallinn, Estonia
gpsr.requests@easproject.com

www.ingramcontent.com/pod-product-compliance
Lightning Source LLC
Chambersburg PA
CBHW052010270326
41929CB00015B/2864